**SECOND
EDITION**

Lost
Found
AND

MORE GREAT BARN FINDS & OTHER AUTOMOTIVE DISCOVERIES

©2011 F+W Media, Inc.

Published by

Our toll-free number to place an order or obtain
a free catalog is (800) 258-0929.

ISBN-13: 978-1-4402-3070-7
ISBN-10: 1-4402-3070-6

Designed by Donna Mummery
Edited by Brian Earnest

Printed in the United States of America

CONTENTS

Hide & Seek

Yes, those barn finds are still out there

How does it continue to happen? How do we keep coming across old cars that have been kept out of sight and out of mind for years, decades and even generations?

It seems impossible that a Duesenberg or Packard or expensive muscle car could have ever been locked away in a shed or barn, or forgotten in a field, and left unmolested for years. Sometimes, they almost hide in plain sight.

But make no mistake, great "barn finds" are still out there — both ordinary, everyman cars and great Classics. Sometimes, they are right under our noses, and all it takes is a phone call, the courage to walk up and knock on the right door, or the luck to "know a guy who knows a guy."

If you're one of those automobile lovers who can't drive by an old garage, barn or shed without thinking to yourself, "I wonder if there's an old car in there?" then this book is for you.

— Brian Earnest

By Angelo Van Bogart

A DEUSY OF A HOT ROD

After being secretly stashed away for more than 60 years, an amazing Duesenberg custom is headed for the street again

This Duesenberg Model A with engine A702 was recently pulled from the California garage where it had rested since 1944. The Duesenberg's chassis was shortened and fitted with a 1928 Chrysler roadster body before 1934. That's a 1931 Graham radiator shell, 1931 Chrysler headlamps and a Lincoln front bumper.

Long before customs cruised with overhead-valve Rocket Eights and hot rods hustled under Ford flathead power, and even earlier than the period when hopped-up Ford Model A four-cylinders began kicking up salt on the flats, there was a different "power of the hour." This power source was derived straight from Indy race cars and installed into passenger cars by 1921. After their time in street cars, many of these used engines were put back into race cars and returned to Indy to add to the legend of

Duesenberg.

Yes, Duesenberg was the source of one of, if not the hottest, powerplant during the 1920s. Its Model A passenger cars of the period used an overhead-cam straight-eight of 260 cubic inches that produced 90-100 hp at 3,000 rpm, good for 90 mph in high gear and 20 mpg — in 1921.

With such power, it's no surprise that Duesenberg passenger car engines were recycled in Indy cars through the early 1930s, and at least one Model A became the foundation for a modified roadster that may just slide the time line back for hot rodding.

"It looks like a high boy," said Randy Ema, an automotive historian and restorer who specializes in Duesenberg, and the owner of the modified Model A roadster shown here.

In November 2010, Ema pulled his shortened, cycle-fendered 1922 Duesenberg roadster out of a Burbank, Calif., garage, where it had rested since 1944.

"I have known of the car for probably 30 years," Ema said. "I used to visit [the owner Wil Johnson] and he actually showed me the car once. He just opened the garage and said, 'Did you see it?' That's how I saw it;

The Duesenberg had been treated like anything but a treasure in its previous life. For years it served as a storage shelf for other miscellaneous garage objects.

The body still retains the charcoal paint and silver moldings that were sprayed in 1934 or earlier, but traces of the Chrysler body's original yellow paint and rumble seat upholstery remain intact.

that was it. He never let me go in."

Ema's view of the Duesenberg was obscured by piles of debris that covered the top of the car in its dark tomb. Since World War II, the car had served as a cumbersome shelf for a baby stroller, golf clubs, cardboard boxes and parts for the other interesting cars Johnson had collected.

"The problem was, he told everyone it was an original Model A roadster, and I think he was afraid to let anybody who knew cars see it," Ema said. "Even his next-door neighbor, who collected [Ford] Model A's, never knew he had cars in there."

During its long slumber, the modified Duesenberg roadster had good company. Its longtime owner had amassed Lincoln Continentals from the 1940s, and at one time, had five Duesenbergs — four Model A's and the Model X Locke-bodied sedan previously featured in *Old Cars Weekly*. When Johnson died about 10 years ago, his family began selling his collection, and until late 2010, all but the Duesenberg roadster had been sold. However, Ema was able to learn much of the car's history from earlier conversations with Johnson and his daughter, and from files of the owner and those Ema has acquired elsewhere.

"[Johnson] was an old engineer and he used to drive this thing to Douglas Aircraft in the 1940s," Ema said. "He bought it in 1934 in Chicago and paid $650 for it from a guy who had a Stutz and Duesenberg business; it was later [John] Troka's dealership in '38 or '39.

"He bought it in June of '34 for $650, and that was more than a Ford. It was probably a fresh car — it had to have looked pretty damn spiffy, and it would have had to for him to pay that kind of money."

Johnson certainly received his money's worth from the Duesenberg. The car provided 10 years of service from 1934 to 1944, which included a drive from Chicago to California. "He drove this one from Chicago, when he came west the first time," Ema said. "We're not sure if it was 1938 or 1940."

After the long drive, the car continued to provide sporting transportation for several more years, through most of World War II. The open-air fun ended in 1944, when the racy car's rear-end apparently went out. It was then parked and never driven again during the 20th century. "When a car broke down, he parked it, he didn't fix it," Ema said of Johnson.

As a restorer, Ema's mission is to make

The Duesenberg retains its original instruments, but the panel behind them was fashioned to fit the Chrysler body.

In November 2010, Ema pulled his shortened, cycle-fendered 1922 Duesenberg roadster out of a Burbank, Calif., garage, where it had rested since 1944.

the roadster drive again, but he's doing his homework before tearing into the car. His first task is determining the components used to modify the car.

"I did know that it was a steel body," Ema said. "I thought for a long time it was a Gardner body. A friend of mine put it on the AACA [forum] and someone said that it's a '28 Chrysler."

With this lead and through his own vast automotive knowledge, Ema has been able to determine the sources for many of the car's other non-Duesenberg components.

"The rear fenders are from the Chrysler roadster, but I don't know what the hood is off," Ema said. "The front fenders, I don't know what they are off, [but] the front bumper is Lincoln. The Model A [Duesenberg] radiator is underneath a 1931 Graham radiator screwed over the top. The headlights are 1931 Chrysler, so I am assuming this car was done in 1932 or '33."

Under the Chrysler body and miscellaneous mixed-make accessories, this "garage find" remains solidly Duesenberg. "The chassis is all Duesenberg, exhaust manifold, brakes, it's all Duesenberg," Ema said.

"It has the brake line and the oil pressure line coming up through [the firewall] to the original Duesenberg instrument panel."

Although the Duesenberg chassis remains with all of its original components, it wasn't spared the torch by the car's original builder. Ema estimates the chassis was shortened at least 10 inches to accommodate the Chrysler roadster body, which replaced a very different style of passenger compartment.

"It was originally a four-passenger touring car," Ema said. "I have the court papers on [Duesenberg's] bankruptcy in 1924, and they list this car in inventory and they call it a four-passenger sport, so I assume it's a four-passenger sport touring."

The engine also received a little hopping up before Johnson purchased it in 1934. The straight-eight's updraft intake manifold was flipped upside down to give the non-stock Winfield carburetor a down-draft arrangement. In the paperwork that accompanied the car, Ema found mention of high-compression pistons which, if installed, won't be uncovered until the engine is torn apart for a rebuild.

"We were going to get it running and pulled the pan and there was 2 inches of sludge," Ema said. "I am going to tear it down soon and get the engine going, and hopefully from there we'll get it back on the road."

Ema is certainly equipped for such an undertaking. Over the years, he's accumulated many of those rare parts removed from cars scrapped from the run of 650 or so Model A Duesenbergs. He also has all of the original Duesenberg drawings, toolings and patterns to restore the biggest Duesenberg basket cases. This car isn't going to get the full treatment, however. In fact, it's more likely to be seen in the future at a cruise-in than a concours.

"You know, I am just going to do the mechanicals and drive it," Ema said. "I probably won't paint it. I may put a top on it, and I am going to put a Model A grille on it. I have a pair of Woodlites I may put on it, but whatever I do, it's not going to hurt it. It would be cost-prohibitive to put the touring body [back] on it."

The "smiles per mile" factor cannot be counted, though, and whether this car is considered an early hot rod or a modified Classic, it will soon happily provide them to enthusiasts of all kinds.

Story and photos by Angelo Van Bogart

FROM PARTS TO PACKARD

Dedicated hobbyist revives Fleetwood-bodied 1924 Packard town car

Although this 1924 Packard Fleetwood-bodied town car probably has just 4,500 miles, it's led an eventful life. It went from a ritzy cabriolet to being cut up for use as a truck to a show beauty.

Don Hanson is among the old car hobby's bravest souls. When he found his 1924 Packard, a First Series Single Eight Fleetwood town car, it was more Packard than Fleetwood. The project was basically a combination between an incomplete 10,001-piece puzzle and a scavenger hunt. However, Hanson wasn't deterred one iota by the car's incomplete and rusty condition when he bought it in 1978.

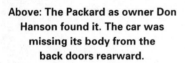

Above: The Packard as owner Don Hanson found it. The car was missing its body from the back doors rearward.

Right: The first step to resurrecting the body was installing new wood.

"I wasn't disappointed, because I didn't know any better," Hanson said. "I had always wanted an early Packard, and for what [restored cars] were selling for, even then, it was more than I felt I could afford. So I was delighted with it."

Hanson was lucky to find the car. When he responded to the ad listing the Packard, he was told it had already been sold. Regardless, he left his phone number with the seller in case the deal fell through. Soon thereafter, Hanson's phone rang and he took off from his Minnesota home to the Upper Peninsula of Michigan to retrieve his prize in the middle of winter.

"Basically, the chassis was complete but the back half of the body had been cut off to make a truck out of it," Hanson said. "Like I learned too many times to count, that was done and people never followed through with it."

When Hanson came upon the car, it was in a state little more than Packard had delivered its chassis to Fleetwood for coachwork. The chassis was complete and the car still carried the radiator, hood, front fenders and instrument panel. Fleetwood's aluminum cowl, front doors and partition between the chauffeur's compartment and rear cabin were also present. However, the rear doors, roof and back portion of the body were lost when a former owner started to make a truck in the 1950s.

"The guy I bought it from lived in Stambaugh, Michigan, and he bought it from the caretaker of the man who originally owned it," Hanson said. "[The seller] just decided it was too ambitious of a project and he threw in the towel.

"Really, it was almost a one-owner car. The original owner, Mr. Richey, was from Chicago," continued Hanson, adding Richey was a president and board chairman of the Chicago Northwestern Railway. "He had a cabin in northern Wisconsin and he took it up there and it was up there its entire life. He died early in the 1950s and he gave it to his caretaker, Otto Leino, and his name

was painted on the door when I got it.

"I was told it was probably in good shape up until the 1950s, when Otto got it and tore the body off [before he returned to his native Norway] and it sat outside."

Though the car was missing part of its body, many of its unique features remained intact. In a nod to his railroad history, the original owner had a red lamp placed on the driver's side running board splash shield and a green lamp on the passenger side. Hanson could also tell the car had originally been painted the same dark green color on the fenders as the body, an atypical fea-

The 1924 Packard Fleetwood-bodied rides on the First Series, Single Eight chassis and has Fleetwood Style No. 2645 coachwork.
Right: Owner Don Hanson.

The instrument panel continues two-tone green paint inside. Gauges include fuel level, oil pressure, amperes, clock and a speedometer.

A jump seat allows for additional passengers in the plush rear compartment.

ture since most Packards of this year had black fenders. The car also has sidemounts, which are very uncommon on 1924 Packards, and the original wheels are optional 20-inch units, rather than the standard 21-inch wheels. As a result, Hanson believes the car was a special-order, and he's certain it's the last Fleetwood town car of its kind.

"It's the only one I know of," he said. "I did find a 1928-'29 [Fleetwood], but I didn't find any earlier ones. It would have been helpful if I could have located other 1924-'25 Fleetwood-bodied Packards to rebuild this car, but I never found any."

The Fleetwood Metal Body Co. was one of many coachbuilders that added to Packard's own already-extensive line of body styles in 1924. The Pennsylvania coachbuilder also supplied bodies to other makes of cars, but Packard was one of Fleetwood's largest customers at the time. Fleetwood had been founded in 1909 in a town of the same name where it built body styles of every configuration, from coupe to sedan to touring to limousine to cabriolet (town car), among others. As was the case with other coachbuilders, Fleetwood bodies were built in runs or to an individual and unrepeated design, and could be trimmed to fit a customer's wishes or the company's own whims.

In 1925, Fleetwood Metal Body Co.'s shareholders sold out to Fisher Body Co., of which General Motors had a controlling stock share since 1919. In 1926, GM took complete control of Fisher in a stock exchange that gave it 100 percent of Fisher's shares. With that trade, Fleetwood Metal Body Co. was completely enveloped into GM, yet Fleetwood continued to produce bodies for other makes of chassis. Soon, General Motors built a satellite plant to Fleetwood in Detroit, then in 1930, all coachwork under the Fleetwood name was completed in Detroit while the Fleetwood, Pa., plant closed.

Despite the number of bodies Fleetwood built, Fleetwood-bodied Packard survivors appear to be rare. With his car's rear section missing, and another Packard project car in the works, Hanson let the 1924 town car project languish. But he didn't stop thinking about the project. He placed advertisements looking for a rear section to the body so he could determine how to correctly reassemble the coachwork. Those ads were never answered, but he never considered parting with the daunting project.

"I really didn't consider selling it, but often times I would contemplate finding another body when I didn't get a response to my ads," Hanson said. "The front section was all complete and otherwise, I probably would have never attempted it. I thought all I had to do was find the rear tub section and doors, and it was a much tougher job than I imagined."

It did help that the Packard's chassis was so complete.

"It was explained to me that it only had

"Basically, the chassis was complete but the back half of the body had been cut off to make a truck out of it," Hanson said. "Like I learned too many times to count, that was done and people never followed through with it."

4,500 miles, which was on the odometer, but the glass [on the gauge] was broken and rusty because it had been sitting outside," he said. "While I wanted to believe that was true, I have no idea of knowing that. The frame and chassis were all intact and it looked very good. It looked complete and not messed with. But it was so rusty, the restoration work was considerable."

Despite its rust, the chassis was a good foundation with which to work. However, Hanson was still missing the rear section, so he began researching how the body should appear. He visited the Detroit Public Library and viewed historic images of similar vehicles, but his big break came in 1988 when he visited Phelps, Wis., the former home of Otto Leino and the vacation home of the Packard's original purchaser.

"I went to back where Otto lived, but first, I had to find out exactly where he lived, so I went to the postmaster in that town," Hanson said. "I asked where Otto Leino lived and found the property was pretty much abandoned. I had driven that far, so I kicked the bushes and looked around and found the

rear section [buried in the dirt]. I only found the bottom half, but I was ecstatic because now I knew the configuration."

Shortly after, another piece fell into place. "Within one month of getting that rear section, this attorney called me and said he had a bunch of rear parts and sections that I could have," Hanson said. "I didn't take a trailer because I didn't expect to get anything, and in the basement of his law office, he had a 1929 or '30 Packard and he had all kinds of parts. There were these two top sections and he gave them both to me. I didn't know which one I wanted to use or which was the best, so I pigeon-holed them in the trunk of my car and took them back home and I had my back half."

A parts sedan was purchased in 1992, which provided the rear doors and other parts. Hanson then delivered the town car's body parts to Gene Irvine of New Madison, Ohio, to have its wood repaired or reconstructed. In 1997, the body and its new wood frame work were returned to Hanson for the fitting of the body panels—a task that proved challenging.

Hanson had a "Daphne at the well" radiator cap from a later Packard fashioned for the car.

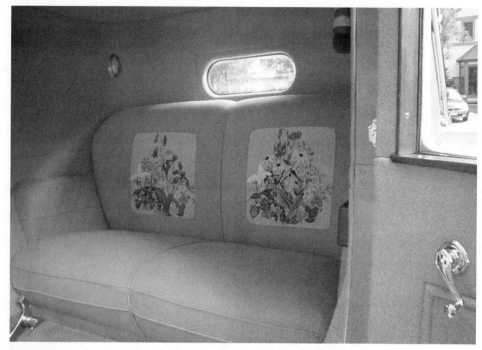

By 2009, the Packard was show-ready inside and out.

Over that winter, Hanson mounted the town car body on the donor car's frame so he could work on the original chassis and the body at the same time. The chassis was cleaned and he prepared to start the engine in the spring.

"Using a beer case for a seat, I towed the car for initial start up," he said. "It fired almost immediately, and within minutes it was running quite well. I drove the chassis, with the beer case seat, around the neighborhood for several trips. The engine ran smoothly — no leaks, no noise from within and no smoke. The engine is also equipped with an air compressor that runs off the transmission. Gotta pump up the tires you know! It also worked perfectly when engaged.

"I still haven't rebuilt the engine and it runs extremely well."

Hanson took the cleaned chassis to Odyssey Restorations in Spring Lake Park, Minn., to be fully restored. The craftsmen at Odyssey Restorations completed mechanical work and dealt with the chassis' rust. In the meantime, Hanson continued fitting the body metal, and when it was completed in 2003, he took the body to Wayne Kempfert of Minneapolis for paint. Hanson chose a light green in place of the original dark green, and its lighter hue has become an attention grabber.

"I was after elegance, and I was after something more bright and cheerful," he said. "I considered gray, but I really wanted to do the green. On this car, I thought it was right and I spent a lot of time sorting out dozens of samples of paint to figure out what it should be. I think it's the color and open front that really grabs people."

By the summer of 2004, the body and sorted-out chassis had been reunited and the Packard was ready to be trimmed. Hanson selected Rick Tillman of R&R Upholstery in White Bear Lake, Minn., to install the roof over the rear compartment. Admittedly, Hanson was particular on how the top should look to remain authentic. He was pleased with the results, so he employed Tillman to upholster the inside.

Left with little clue how the interior originally looked on his Fleetwood-bodied Packard, Hanson and Tillman relied on period photos uncovered in the Detroit Public Library's collection to upholster the car.

Meanwhile, the 85-hp, 357.8-cid straight-eight registered low oil pressure and had water jackets that leaked, so with the prodding of a fellow Packard enthusiast, Hanson continued to tweak the engine. He now knows his car's engine front to back

and how to properly tune it.

"I should have put zippers on the oil pan and front cover, I had them off and on so many times," he said.

By 2009, the car was ready to be shown, and it made appearances at concours such as the Milwaukee Masterpiece and Salisbury Concours d'Elegance, plus two Classic Car Club of America meets, where its received its Primary and Senior Awards, which confirm its authenticity. Hanson also hopes to enter the car in Antique Automobile Club of America events in the future.

"I would really like to take it to Hershey in October and that's a big commitment," he said. "When I took it to the Masterpiece, I got the Most Elegant Award, and I usually get some kind of an award. It's nice to get an award, but I enjoy the show for the show."

Through the years, Hanson has sold cars in order to start new projects, but this Packard might just be a keeper. "I would like to think I won't sell it, but we're all just caretakers. It's the journey — not the destination — that drives us," he said.

Maybe there is another Packard puzzle waiting around the corner. And if there is, Hanson is just the man to put it back together.

By Angelo Van Bogart

MILESTONE MODEL A
Landmark Ford went undercover for many years

The long-lost 20th millionth Ford — a 1931 Model A — has become celebrity again, just as it was when it rolled off the Ford assembly line.

In the fall of 2000, one of the most historic and presumed lost Fords of all time was unearthed from 40 years of storage in a garage in Michigan's Upper Peninsula. The 20 Millionth Ford, a black 1931 Model A Town Sedan, is not only important from the numeric assignment given to it on the assembly line, but for the dignitaries that used it while Ford promoted the car around the country.

After a few publicity shots were taken of the landmark Ford after it rolled off the assembly line, none other than Henry Ford drove the Model A Ford off the assembly line and into history books. Henry's son, Edsel, who is credited for making the Mod-

A rear view of the 1931 Model A Town Sedan reveals the "The Twenty Millionth Ford" writing on its spare tire cover. Ford Motor Company Chief of Staff John Rintamaki explained that, "Henry wanted people to make sure they could read it," so he put the car's numeric designation on every side, including the car's roof.

el A the beautiful automobile that it is, was in the passenger seat.

"Ford made it important when Henry Ford stamped the number on the block and drove it off the assembly line," Rod Liimatainen said. His family has owned the 20 Millionth Ford since 1940, when Ford Motor Co. initially sold the car.

From the Rouge assembly plant, Henry Ford drove the car to his home where he and the Model A Ford were photographed with Henry's first car, the Quadricycle. From there, the landmark car was driven by Col. C.D. Hilton on a promotional tour where it received honors from Americans across the country.

"It went on a nationwide tour and thousands, if not millions, saw it," Liimatainen said.

The car's first stop in New York found it honored with a drive by Mayor James Walker, who met the car at the steps of city hall. Even Eleanor Roosevelt drove the car when it stopped by the New York governor's house, where her husband held office.

In Texas, the car was photographed with the town of Brady's 20 millionth turkey as a crowd looked on. Many states honored the

When Liimatainen's father bought the car, he had full knowledge of the car's star-studded past despite the fact Ford had tried to brush away the car's past by painting over the giant white lettering that proclaimed the car's heritage.

car with "20000000" license plates while the people of the Sioux Nation induced the car as a member of their tribe. The car was driven by many dignitaries between, such as actor/producer Douglas Fairbanks, champion golfer Glenna Collett and Admiral Richard E. Byrd, among others.

Through its tour, the 20 Millionth Ford racked miles from New York to the West Coast, then to the south and finally back to Dearborn, Mich. Once home, it was housed in Dearborn's Ford Museum for 10 years. After its decade-long stay, Ford sold the special Town Sedan to current owner Rod Liimatainen's father for $550, just $80 less than the model's original $630 base price. When Liimatainen's father bought the car, he had full knowledge of the car's star-studded past despite the fact Ford had tried to brush away the car's past by painting over the giant white lettering that proclaimed the car's heritage.

Although the non-descript Model A putted around the Liimatainens' Upper Peninsula hometown looking as ordinary as any other Model A, a few local Ford fans were keen to its identity and importance, but kept its secret for decades.

"It was known in the area," Liimatainen said. "A lot of people wanted to buy it over the years."

Liimatainen's parents knew the car was of historic value, and after the elder Liimatainen's death, his wife and son preserved it. "I thought it was my duty to save the car," Liimatainen said.

After his father passed on the car to Liimatainen and is mother in the 1950s, it never left the garage.

"I drove it when I was 16 and almost wrecked it," he said. "I did not trust myself [with the car]."

Ford had masked the car's past well. Although the Liimatainens knew what they had, others remained skeptical until its restoration began in the 2000.

"Somebody had painted it a few times," Terry Deter of Deters Restorations in Temperence, Ohio, said. "I wasn't 100 percent sold on it."

Based on the shop's award-winning work on other Model A's, Deters Restorations was selected to restore the car by the car's owner and Ford Motor Co., which helped fund the project.

"The story I got was Ford sanded the paint before they sold it," Deter said. This made it difficult to determine if the long-lost car had, indeed, been found.

Ford historian Bob Kreipke investigated the car's existence in 2000 and tracked it to Liimatainen's mother's garage in the Upper Peninsula. There, he found a dusty Model A that had been parked for more than 40 years with about 50,000 miles on its odometer.

After Kreipke determined the car was legitimate, Henry Ford's great-grandson William Clay Ford II stopped to see the car in the Liimatainens' garage before it was shipped out for a body-off-frame restoration funded at least in part by the auto industry giant.

"As far as I understand, [William Clay Ford II] went up to… see the car," Deter said. Ford was also filmed with the car at his home for a documentary on the Model A that Ford was in the process of producing.

After Ford's visit, the car was completely torn apart. "The bare frame is sitting against the wall," Deters said at the time of the restoration. "It's being put back the way it came off the assembly line."

Deters said the car arrived in his shop in relatively good original condition with most of the original upholstery and very little rust.

"It's not an easy restoration, but not a difficult one," Deters said. "It certainly, for the most part, was all there."

Helpng preserve the body were at least two coast of paint over the original black coat. A close initial inspection by Deters showed no signs of the lettering on the car's sides or roof. He was doubtful of the car's history until the disassembly began. When he took the frame of the car off, he found the magic serial number — A20000000.

"The body has never been off the frame," Deters added, a sure sign that the car remained unmolested and the Liimatainen's story had held up.

Further proof of the car's authenticity came when the Deters began stripping the paint and found primer between coats of paint where the lettering should have been.

Deters Restorations spent about a year restoring the car. When it was completed, the car made its debut at the 2002 Iola Old Car Show, which featured the 1928-'31 Ford Model A, then was displayed at Ford Motor Co. headquarters for, ironically, another 10 years.

Story and photos by Bill Rothermel, SAH

THE NEIGHBORLY LASALLE

1934 convertible coupe serves as a faithful companion

34-year-old Wade Tibbitts noticed this 1934 LaSalle languishing in a neighbor's garage when he was a child. Tibbitts and his father purchased the car in 2010, made it operable and immediately began taking it to shows.

In the late 1920s, companion cars were all the rage at General Motors. Buick had Marquette; Oldsmobile offered Viking; Oakland featured Pontiac; and Cadillac, the LaSalle. By 1932, both Marquette and Viking had been dropped; Oakland, too, as it was usurped by Pontiac, its understudy. Inside GM, there was talk of dropping LaSalle, which had been legendary design director Harley Earl's baby as his first project for GM. However, LaSalle sales had dropped from a high of 22,961 in 1929 to 3,386 in 1932 and 3,482 in 1933, fueling the argument to abandon the marque. The struggling early-'30s economy made it tough to sell automobiles, especially upstarts such

The rear view is all Tibbitts had of the LaSalle for many years. He didn't get a view of the art deco instrument panel until he and his father called the car their own.

as LaSalle.

Earl's solution was to present the LaSalle as an all-new car for 1934. Styled by Jules Agramonte under the tutelage of Earl, the new LaSalle was nothing short of sensational. Backed by the prestige of Cadillac with bodies by Fleetwood, the LaSalle was priced $1,000 less than the least-expensive Cadillac in order to compete for buyers in the upper-medium price range. Styling was streamlined featuring a slender V radiator, teardrop headlamps, circular ports arrayed in a vertical line along the hood, chevrons on the front fenders and unique-for-1934 bi-plane bumpers — all very art deco features. Bendix hydraulic brakes were Cadillac's first use of the new technology and were only used on LaSalles for 1934. A new 240-cid, 95-hp L-head straight-eight for the La-Salle was built by Oldsmobile to Cadillac's specifications. The fact that all LaSalles were legitimately assembled by the crafts-man at GM's Fleetwood body works cer-tainly added to the cachet. The division sold 7,218 cars for the year, more than doubling that of the previous year.

Lawrence Fisher, president of Cadillac, first noticed Earl in 1925 when he was de-signing custom coachwork in Hollywood. About the same time, General Motors presi-dent Alfred P. Sloan, Jr. wished to fill the price gap in GM's lineup between Buick and Cadillac. The new LaSalle became the car to fill it and Earl was hired to design the coachwork on a consulting basis.

"Not quite as conservative as the Cadil-lac," was the instruction given Earl, and he chose the Hispano-Suiza as his inspiration. The LaSalle was introduced to much ac-claim on March 5, 1927 – a full 15 models on two wheelbases ranging in price from $2,495 to $4,700. By year's end, 16,850 had been sold and Earl had a full-time job at GM as head of the newly created Art and Colour Section.

The LaSalle is memorable not for its engineering, but rather its styling, and Earl was the man responsible. The LaSalle was a smash hit when it was introduced in 1927. One reporter wrote that it was ". . . just about the most beautiful car he had ever seen."

Wade Tibbitts, a 34-year-old collector in Salt Lake City, Utah, agrees.

"The car belonged to a neighbor of ours," recalled Tibbitts of his 1934 LaSalle. "I can remember as a child riding my bike around and seeing the back end of that red car peek-ing out of the garage. At a really young age, I made my dad drag me to all the car shows, but I had no idea what I was looking at. I got more into cars as I got older. When I was in my teens and my parents were on vacation, I drug my first engine home from the junk yard. I kind of forced my dad into a partner-ship." The engine belonged to a 1956 Chev-rolet that Tibbitts would later restore.

The neighbor who owned the LaSalle came over quite often to talk during the restoration of the '56 Chevy and remarked to the (then) teenager that he wanted to get

his car out and running, too.

"We walked over to look at the car and that is when I discovered it was a LaSalle," Tibbitts said. "My grandparents had a 1937 LaSalle, so I was kind of familiar with the name. I knew it was something special, but I still had no idea the significance of what it was until much later when I started getting into Classic cars."

The known history of the car goes back to the early 1960s. The car was purchased by a prominent local judge who was an avid collector. Upon his passing, a son inherited the car. The son was Tibbitt's neighbor. He, too, would pass on. While helping the neighbor's widow repair her garage door, Tibbitts and his father suggested she have the car professionally appraised. "This is the first time I got to see the car with educated eyes. I was stunned how complete and rust-free it was," Tibbitts said. Lo and behold, a deal was struck and the car was purchased by the father-and-son duo in June 2010.

Underneath a layer of dust was a remarkable survivor of the Classic era. In addition to the lack of rust, there was no significant wood rot in the frame. Save for a red-and-black repaint dating to the 1960s over its original Diana Crème exterior, the car was a remarkable survivor of the scant 600 LaSalle convertible coupes produced for 1934.

"Even the tires were aired up," Tibbitts said. "Unfortunately, mice and rats made a

The LaSalle is memorable not for its engineering, but rather its styling, and Earl was the man responsible.

meal out of the carpeting. But overall, it was in amazing condition."

The brake pedal went completely to the floor when depressed, so it was obvious the brake system would need to be addressed. According to the prior owner, the car was taken to a mechanic with the idea of getting it running. It was started, but brought home and never run again. To this day, the LaSalle still wears the inspection sticker from its last registration period — dated 1965!

The parts required to fix the brakes ar-

rived just three days before the Utah Concours d'Elegance on Aug. 28, 2010, where the LaSalle was to make its debut. Remarkably, the car was put back together and ready for the show.

Prior to the Tibbittses purchasing the car, it had only been driven 200 miles since 1964, as evidenced by an oil change sticker on the inside of the door from a local gas station. Today, the odometer reads 80,077 miles.

The Series 350 convertible coupe was

one of four LaSalle models offered for 1934, all riding a 119-inch wheelbase. Designated Model 6335, the convertible coupe seated two or four passengers, depending upon whether or not the rumble seat was used. Weighing in at 3,780 lbs., base price was $1,695. Most people became acquainted with the 1934 LaSalle convertible coupe when Bill Rader paced the 1934 Indianapolis 500 in one such car.

LaSalle production continued through 1940, when Cadillac called it quits due to LaSalle's declining sales. For 1941, Cadillac re-introduced the Series 61 to replace the LaSalle as the price leader in its lineup.

Tibbitts hopes to find some of the missing pieces such as the bumpers, the original air cleaner and the ashtrays in the doors to make the car complete.

"Other than the color change, it is intact as it was built," Tibbitts said. As for his plans for the car, Tibbitts said, "I'm going to leave well enough alone. This is an incredible time capsule."

As in 1934, some 75 years earlier, this LaSalle remains a faithful companion, albeit for a younger generation.

Story by Angelo Van Bogart
Photos courtesy of Mike Hendel and Barry Dosdall

REGAL RIDE

Grace Vanderbilt's unique Rollston-bodied 1934 Packard town 'essentially disappeared'

Many Rollston bodies feature the V-windshield, but this is the only known 1934 Packard incorporating the styling element. The sharp and very formal lines to the town car coachwork still harmonize with the smooth shapes of the Packard fenders, hood and radiator.

With the last name "Vanderbilt," Grace Wilson Vanderbilt couldn't be seen in anything less than a Packard. The family of her husband, Cornelius Vanderbilt III, had built its fortune on transportation — first ferries, then railroads — so moving and shaking was in the family blood. By Grace Vanderbilt's lifetime, the shaking evolved to hobnobbing with high society and royalty, and the moving came courtesy of Packard.

Several photographs from the 1910s and 1920s show Vanderbilts at the running boards of contemporary Packards, so Grace didn't need to ask a man who owned one when she went car shopping in the late 1930s. Her hunt took her to an unusual Rollston-bodied Packard that had originally escorted fellow "Old Knickerbocker Society" socialite Mrs. Allen A. Ryan. Ryan had purchased the Rollston Packard from the stock of Park Avenue Packard, a Packard Motor Car Co. of New York distributor not far from the Park Avenue mansion Vanderbilt shared with her husband in New York City. Although it was certainly unusual for one as wealthy as Grace Vanderbilt to buy a second-hand automobile, the Rollston Packard was still worthy of a notable socialite, and definitely unique in high society.

"It's an Eight chassis, which is odd, because, the story that seems to flow on this car is that it was sold at Park Avenue Packard, and nobody needed the big long wheelbase and power to get around the city," said Tom Laferriere of the Rollston town car-bodied 1934 Packard Eight he recently purchased. Laferriere uncovered the town car from decades of storage after receiving a tip on its whereabouts from Packard historian Jim Pearsall.

Although it was certainly unusual for one as wealthy as Grace Vanderbilt to buy a second-hand automobile, the Rollston Packard was still worthy of a notable socialite, and definitely unique in high society.

"It is uncommon, and I think where you would find it was in New York City, because of the volume of traffic," Pearsall said. "They could have put the same coachwork on an 1108 chassis, and there was a beautiful 1108 Rollston town car in 1934, but around New York City with heavy traffic, the Super Eight or Eight chassis would have been better."

In 1934, Packard offered three series of its Eleventh Series model: the Eight, Super Eight and Twelve. The Eight had a smaller displacement straight-eight compared to its larger companions, as well as wheelbases in shorter increments. However, the Packard Eight's 319.2 cubic inches supplied plenty of power in the city, and the wheelbases in 129-1/2-, 136-1/4- and 141-1/2-inch lengths gave it a tighter turning radius for navigating the cramped quarters of New York City during the Great Depression. As logical as this may seem, it was rare for a coachwork as formal as a town car to be fitted to the Eight chassis, even though most town cars were sold in large cities.

"There's a lot of speculation why it was done," Laferriere said. "It was done when it was new; obviously, it's not a body swap."

Of the Rollston town cars known to have been built for Packard chassis in 1934, the Ryan-Vanderbilt car is the only known survivor.

"This Rollston has a split windshield and to my understanding, Rollston made two of these town car bodies in '34," Laferriere said. "One was on an 1108 chassis and it's got a flat windshield."

Although their windshield designs vary, both known Rollston-bodied 1934 Packards have sharp edges to their respective passenger compartments that provide a very formal look, and each carries the deeply skirted front fenders flanking the vertical radiator that define Packards of this year. However, the Rollston town car counterpart to Laferriere's Packard is mounted on the Twelve-cylinder 1108 chassis on the 146-7/8-inch wheelbase — Packard's longest that year.

It's possible Rollston only built two

Years of outdoor storage have taken their toll on the interior of the Packard. Although it appears original and intact, it will require restoration.

town cars on the Packard chassis in 1934, because the traditional body style was considered haughty in the depths of the Great Depression. Additionally, Packard already cataloged two LeBaron town cars, so most buyers would have simply ordered Packard's recommended coachwork. However, this Rollston town car would have been more readily apparent to the New York City socialites since New York City-based Rollston had built the car on spec and displayed it at Park Avenue Packard, thus eliminating the wait for a cataloged LeBaron to be built. And, for the wealthiest of socialites, the green-and-black Packard Rollston town car was not only the right make and body style, but even the appropriate color.

"Most Vanderbilt cars were maroon and black, but this one was green," Laferriere said. "It's the color of money."

Grace Vanderbilt passed away in 1953, so it's impossible to determine if the color swayed her purchase. However, it's not surprising she didn't adhere to the family's use of red and black, given the fact her husband had been disinherited by his father, Cornelius Vanderbilt II, for their union. Even though fences were eventually mended with her husband's mother, Grace would never own a Packard in the trademark Vanderbilt colors, as this green-and-black Packard would be her calling card through the remainder of her life.

"She used this car until 1951," Laferriere said. "Just picture that for a minute — she was still being driven around in this car when 1951 Chevrolets were new."

Today, the Packard remains largely unrestored and still wears that green-and-black paint scheme. Like many chauffeur-driven town cars, it was well cared for during its years of service, and those years were many. From what Laferriere can tell, the car remained well-preserved for most of its life, although today, it is in need of restoration.

"It was in storage from 1951 to 1961," Laferriere said. "After Grace Vanderbilt died, the car, through her son, was donated in 1957 to the Abyssinian Baptist Church. They never licensed it and it remained in dead storage. The church sold the car in February 1961 to C. Kornorf. Then it was purchased in 1968 by the [Mead] family I bought it from."

Before its 1968 sale to the Mead family, the '34 Packard Eight Rollston town car was well-known by Packard enthusiasts. Once the Meads took ownership, the car fell out of view.

"The car essentially disappeared," Pearsall said. "It was known to have been in Florida in the early '70s and then it disappeared and people wondered what happened to that car. I got wind of it last summer and started to track it down."

Pearsall shared his discovery with Laferriere, who made contact with the Mead family.

"The daughter would talk about how she was always riding in the car and they

This wire photograph taken on New York City's Fifth Avenue upon the opening of the Bache Art Collection in 1937 is believed to also show the Rollston-bodied Vanderbilt 1934 Packard town car.

went on all of these rides, so they were using it," Laferriere said. The fun was short-lived, because the registrations stopped in the 1970s when the Packard was parked again, left to fall out of the microscope of the hobby. During this bout of storage, father time was not so kind.

When Laferriere viewed the car, it had clearly suffered the ravages of outdoor storage. He did what any enthusiast who stumbles onto an historic car would do and began negotiating its purchase to preserve the weathering car.

"The family wanted to keep it, but there was a storage war and the warehouse owner ended up putting it outside, and that is what destroyed it," Laferriere said.

After a deal was struck, Laferriere added it to his Packard-heavy collection. Since purchasing it, he has been combing over its condition and features.

"It's almost all there, but it is missing the radiator cap, air cleaner and the Packard ornament, because that is easily stolen," he said.

"I get a thrill of getting them started and running and making everything work again," he said. "I had it running, but it will need a full restoration. It needs paint, chrome, interior, but the [engine] sounds pretty good. I am going to keep working towards detailing the mechanics of the car."

While Laferriere is excited about the car, he feels it should undergo a full restoration by another enthusiastic Packard collector. He plans to add the car to the inventory of his business, Laferriere Classic Cars.

"I want to share the car and let the next person take it to that level of restoration," Laferriere said.

He feels the next owner will have a unique opportunity to own a slice of history.

"I call this the find of the century, because you don't find custom-bodied cars that often, especially at this point in time in the hobby. This car has two things going for it: It has the automotive history, because it's a Rollston '34 Packard, but it also has American [Vanderbilt] history tied to it, as well."

By Angelo Van Bogart

COMEBACK CUSTOM

Long-lost '37 Ford coupe is a star, again

Glenn Johnson built this 1937 Ford custom from 1947-'51, all the while driving it to work every day. The car landed on the cover of *Hot Rod Magazine* in 1952.

Examples from Joe Bortz's collection of factory-built concept cars from the 1950s and '60s have appeared on the pages of *Old Cars Weekly* for decades. So it shouldn't be surprising that he also has a soft spot for customs that hail from the same era.

"In a vague way, there is a relationship between custom cars and concept cars," Bortz said. "The customs that are really done right are like some concept cars. The General Motors Tech Center would do the same thing sometimes — take a production car off the line and their teams of designers and engineers would modify it to come up with a concept car."

In Bortz's opinion, the Glenn Johnson 1937 Ford coupe custom, his latest of four

custom cars, has the quality and even the popularity of those production-based concept cars from their heyday.

"I think the architectural design of the Johnson car speaks for itself," Bortz said. "Most guys that customized cars were modifying them; they were taking off the hood ornament and they are exchanging tail lights, but they are not taking into perspective the overall package. I think Glen Johnson was one of the first guys who considered the overall design and worked backwards. He didn't just cut and make nips here and there."

Hot Rod Magazine agreed, and in 1952 it put Johnson's chopped-and-channeled 1937 Ford on the cover of its April issue. Inside the issue, Johnson explained how he turned his daily driver into a cover car between 1947-'51, all the while driving it 60 miles back and forth to work six days a week.

As a future architect, Johnson had the skills at the time to map out his channel and chop job. He sketched out the profile of his 1937 coupe — a car he called an "ugly duckling" — then determined the new, lower profile of his coupe. His sketch included a rake to the windshield and repositioning the rear fenders slightly forward and higher as a result of the slight shift in the location of the body after its channeling. He also designed a pointier prow and 1940 Ford headlamp bezels.

Since this was to be his first attempt at

Johnson mounted all the gauges above the windshield and had the panel beneath the windshield upholstered. The car carries a 1947 Mercury flathead with two carburetors and other early-1950s speed equipment.

"I think Glen Johnson was one of the first guys who considered the overall design and worked backwards. He didn't just cut and make nips here and there."

major body work, let alone a chop-and-channel job, Johnson studied a friend's chopped-and-channeled 1936 Ford coupe, but it offered few clues.

"The first thing I did was to thoroughly examine [Carl Ganz's] '36, hoping to pick up ideas, but due to outstanding workmanship, the secrets of its reconstruction methods remained as mysterious as the ancient Sphinx," Johnson said in his *Hot Rod Magazine* article. Johnson also consulted "experts," none of which provided enlightening advice, so he drove the car under a shade tree in the backyard of his Las Vegas home and got to work with some basic body tools and borrowed welding equipment.

After measuring and planning, he chopped the top, filled the gaps with new metal and then leaded over the welds and other body work. Next came the body channeling, which dropped the body about 6 inches on the frame. Johnson removed the fenders, running boards, hood, grille and deck lid before dropping the body. He sliced and diced areas of the body, including the firewall and the rear wheel openings, to accommodate the lowering of the

body on the chassis. All the while, the Ford was serving daily driver duty, sometimes with major body parts missing!

After the channel was completed, Johnson molded the rear fenders into the body, the set out to re-fit the front clip on the channeled body. The nose of the Ford car was heavily reshaped with a 1947 Cadillac grille, capped by a 1941 Cadillac front bumper. Meanwhile, a split 1946 De Soto rear bumper was fitted in the rear.

It took Johnson a year to complete the lead work and file the weld marks on the body before the car was finally painted, the glass re-fitted and the body trimmed. Then, just one week after all this work was completed, disaster struck. In his article, Johnson said a smoldering rag ignited the gas tank and blistered the paint, cracked the glass and destroyed the interior. While devastated at the time, Johnson looked back on the event as an opportunity to perfect the skills he developed during the car's initial build. Much of the work that took him hours the first time was reduced to minutes.

In the end, Johnson's 1937 Ford turned

The coupe was well known on the California show scene in the 1950s, but then disappeared from the public.

out to be a show-stopping creation. After its cover appearance, the car is known to have appeared at the Pasadena Auto Show. According to Bortz, the car was shown for three years, then it suddenly disappeared from the scene.

"He bought that car in '47 and finished it in '50-'51, showed it through '52-'55 and then parked it next to his desert home in Nevada, and for 40 years, it just sat there."

The dry desert climate helped preserve the custom Ford, but after decades of baking in the hot Nevada sun while the car was parked behind a building, it needed a restoration. By the early 2000s, Johnson had rebuilt his 1937 Ford — for the third time — completing everything himself except the upholstery.

After that, he began showing it again. "After he restored it to the condition as he first built it, he put it in one show before he died," Bortz said. Bortz acquired Johnson's coupe around 2007 and had a few finishing touches completed to make the car appear exactly as it did for the 1952 *Hot Rod Magazine* cover.

"When I got it, the only thing that was missing were the fender skirts, so Fran Roxas made a set of fender skirts and he detailed the engine compartment," Bortz said. "[Johnson] had put a modern tape deck in the dash and we pulled it out and put back in an early-1950s radio front."

Apparently, Johnson had hoped to take the coupe to more shows following its restoration, and Bortz is trying to honor that legacy. "His wish was it would go to somebody who would show it again, and I said I would see that the car got exhibited in a meaningful way, and that is what happened. It's been a lot of fun."

So far, Bortz has shown the car at the 2011 Grand National Roadster Show. It's scheduled to appear at the 2011 Detroit Autorama. Fans of well-done customs will have another chance to check out this handsome custom at the 2011 Amelia Island Concours d'Elegance.

By Angelo Van Bogart

THE EIFEL FORD

Restored roadster is unique and rare German immigrant

This 1937 Eifel roadster came to the U.S. in the 1950s, but was then taken off the road for many years before recently making a comeback.

It took nearly 55 years, but Manny Feijoo's Ford Eifel experience came full circle at the AACA's 2010 Eastern Fall Meet in Hershey, Pa.

In 1956, the Johnson City, N.Y., resident saw an Eifel for the first time at the Hershey event. In 1987, Feijoo saw his second Eifel when he was approached about storing a tiny roadster. Although he didn't have space for such a project, he was interested in learning more about the car.

"My antenna went up and I made an appointment to look at it," he recalled upon learning about the 1937 Eifel roadster.

we can split the cost of the appraisal.'"

The asking price turned out to be reasonable, and in 1987, Feijoo found himself the owner of the second Eifel he'd ever spotted — a 1937 roadster project car. Twenty-three years later, in 2010, Feijoo drove that 1937 Eifel roadster onto the Hershey show field for the first time, just days after finally completing the restoration.

Ford built the Eifel in Köln, Germany, and in Hungary from 1935 to just 1940, under Adolf Hitler's control of Germany. That historical fact affected how the car was built, and partially explains its brief life.

All of the parts of the Köln-built Eifel denote their country of origin as Germany. "Hitler wanted all the parts made in Germany," said Feijoo. "All of the parts have the Ford script... the muffler hanger, the lug nuts..." in addition to the country of origin.

"The brother of the previous owner said if he didn't find a place to store it, he'd sell it. I asked for first right of refusal and six months later, he called to sell the car."

Given its age and imported status, Feijoo found it difficult to put a dollar amount on the unusual car.

"He wanted an offer, but I told him I didn't know what it was worth," Feijoo said. "I said, 'Let's have an appraisal, and if I can afford it, I will buy the car. If not,

Despite its German heritage, the roadster definitely has the Ford look, from its wind-splitting V-shaped grille to its skirted fenders. While restoring the car, Feijoo immediately discovered the Eifel's relationship to American Ford products.

"I did the chassis when I first got it," he

The Ford Eifel is powered by a 1.2-liter four-cylinder capable of 34 hp. There were just 42,000 miles on the engine when owner Manny Feijoo purchased the car in 1987.

said. "It's a miniature Ford underneath."

The Eifel actually shares the smaller Model C platform of British Anglias and Prefects of the period, which likewise borrowed from the American Ford chassis design, albeit on a smaller scale. Like the British Fords, the Eifel was powered by a four-cylinder engine, the Eifel unit being of 1.2 liters in displacement and 34 hp. Feijoo said the four-cylinder in his Eifel hadn't traveled more than 42,000 miles before the car was imported to the United States in the 1950s.

"I bought it in '87 from the brother of the man who brought it home from the service in the '50s," he said. "I recently had a conversation with the gentleman's brother, and he said before they shipped the car [to the United States], his parents and brother drove the car to Amsterdam." Given the Eifel roadster's size and two-passenger status, it must have been one cramped cruise!

Once the car landed on American shores, the Eifel's travels appear to have halted. However, the car remained intact and well preserved.

"It was probably 95 to 98 percent original and complete with no rust," Feijoo said.

Eifels aren't common in the United States, so having one in relatively good condition and complete certainly worked in Feijoo's favor. "I used [nearly] all the

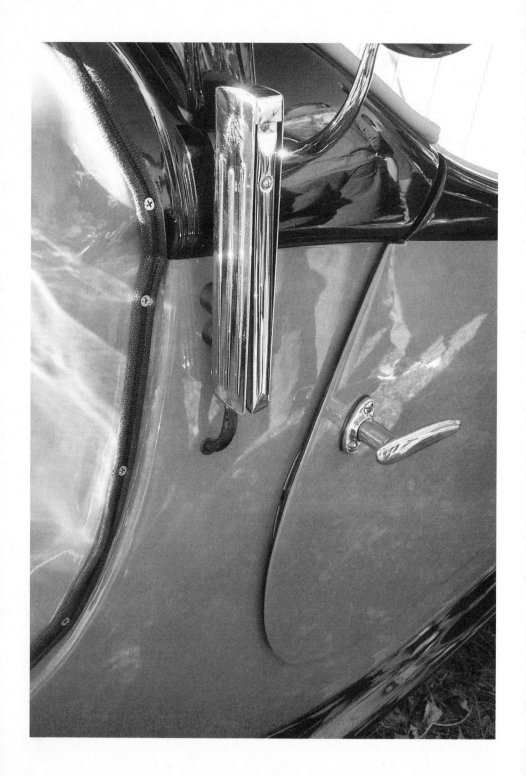

"The brother of the previous owner said if he didn't find a place to store it, he'd sell it. I asked for first right of refusal and six months later, he called to sell the car."

original parts," Feijoo said. That included re-using parts such as the original fuel lines, because the proper size was not available in the United States. In other cases, unique Eifel parts had to be made to put the car in show condition.

"Some of the wood [in the body] was replaced," said Feijoo, whose skills as a tool and die maker helped prepare him for the undertaking of restoring a rare car located a long way from home. "I had to make latches for the roof, a horn bezel, dash insert, all the fasteners and even the key.

"There were 23 teeth missing from the flywheel. I tig-welded then milled teeth after teeth, then hardened and tempered the teeth and ground all of them."

The tail lamps were among the few missing parts. After spending years collecting literature and photos of Ford Eifels during his extensive research, Feijoo was able to determine the correct appearance and size of the lamps. He also noticed they were very similar to American 1934 Ford tail lamps, so he modified a set from a U.S.-built Ford by lengthening them to the proper size. The result is tail lamps that look as though they have been with the car since day one.

Adding into the rarity is the car's body style. Feijoo said out of the 62,000 Eifels built from 1935-'40, just a handful were roadsters.

"Stoewer, Karmann and Graber built about 100 roadsters for Ford, and it's possibly one of six [roadsters] left," he said.

The remaining Eifels were two-door sedans, cabriolets and similarly diminutive trucks. In 1937, Feijoo said Eifels were available in nine color schemes, and as a two-seat roadster from 1937, his Eifel has some unique features for the model year.

"1937 is the only year for cut-down doors," he noted.

Feijoo did more than make new parts during the Eifel's restoration — he also completed much of the other work himself, leaving only the paint, upholstery and wiring harness to other professionals.

Feijoo expects to have some fun with his little restored rarity. "I intend to drive it a little bit and enjoy it," Feijoo said. "I've put about 100 miles on it, and it will do 60 mph. It handles and rides well, but it's a little short on brakes."

WAITING ON A FRIEND

1938 Chevy is no longer a prisoner

Richard Thomas first saw his 1938 Chevrolet when he was a teen. Four decades later he pulled it from a shed and restored it.

Richard Thomas waited a long time to land his "Sweetie." More than four decades in fact. And when opportunity finally knocked, even at the least-expected time and most unlikely place, he didn't hesitate.

Thomas had known about the 1938 Chevrolet Master Business Coupe since he and the car's owner were childhood friends back in the 1960s. Even though he didn't own other collector cars and wasn't active in the car hobby, Thomas had always told his friend, Mike Webb, that he'd like to buy his car someday. He was always rebuffed, until his luck finally began to change in late 2003. The two man bumped into each other at a garage sale after not seeing each other for many years, and Thomas again gave Webb his sales pitch. A year later, Thomas called him on the phone, still pining for the car. Then, finally, in December of 2004, the pair saw each other at another garage sale, and this time, Webb's tune had changed.

"I think he had hoped and hoped that he'd get around to restoring it, but his health was getting bad," said Thomas, a resident of Arkansas City, Kansas. "Life isn't always fair, and it wasn't fair to him. He was having some hard times.

"But I was very surprised that he agreed to sell it to me. I could hardly believe it."

It would seem no great surprise that Webb would have trouble parting with the car he had owned for so many years. He had gotten the car from the original owner, Elijah Ham, who had purchased the car new from a fledgling dealership in Arkansas City. Ham, a friend of the Webb family, apparently drove the car very little, and during his retirement years decided to give the car to Mike Webb, who was just 14 at the time. Thomas says the other boys didn't know Webb even had such a car, but he remembers the day everyone found out!

"The first first time I saw it just a bunch of us guys 17, 18 years old, right in that area, we were just hanging out and doing what teenagers did in the '60s," he said. "I didn't even know he had it. I about died when I saw it. It was just a cool old car. Of course, we didn't really know much about it, I just thought it was cool.

The car hadn't seen the sunshine in more than 20 years when it was dragged out of a shed.

"He let us all drool, then took it back to the house. He'd get it out on occasion. But he eventually had a little problem with the brakes — the positive battery cable rubbed

The engine eventually stuck, the interior was shot, thanks in part to varmints, and the the body needed a lot of work, but the 1938 coupe was worth saving for Thomas.

a hole in the brake line. And one day he popped the brakes and ran into the back of a flatbed truck and put a nice crease in the grille. After that he rolled her into the barn and there she sat …

"It just stayed in the barn and as time went on we both went our own ways and didn't much of each other. … Every once in a while we'd pass ways and I'd kind of half-heartedly say, "Hey, want to sell me that car yet?"

By the time Thomas got his chance to own the car, which he calls his "Sweetie," it had sat for more than 20 years. The gas had turned "to varnish" and the neglected Chevy was covered with a thick layer of dust. It had also become home to genera-tions of unidentified varmints and various other creatures. It was a long way from the impressive, shiny coupe that Thomas remembered from his teenage years.

"I was kind of hoping it would be in kind of shape where it had been setting for a while, but wasn't let go as much as it had been," he said. "I was hoping to change the oil, put a fresh battery in it and go for a ride. But that was not the case."

Chevrolet's "diamond crown" styling changes were introduced for the 1937 models and carried over into 1938. The changes included safety glass in all the windows and fenders that were straight on the sides. The '38s had a new grilled that alternated narrow and wide hori-zontal bars with a center molding down

There were a total of 12 different Chevrolets available in 1938 — six each in both the Master and Master Deluxe lineups.

the middle. There were a few other styling tweaks for the '38s, but the body shells and running boards were the same on the '37s and '38s.

The hoods had ventilators with three chrome horizontal moldings. The headlights were bullet-shaped and mounted close to the grille. Master series cars — there was also a higher-end Master Deluxe series — hand single tail lamps.

Under the hood was the familiar Chevy inline six, displacing 216.5 cid and producing a modest 85 hp. A three-speed manual transmission with the stick on the floor was standard on all the bowtie '38s.

There were a total of 12 different Chevrolets available in 1938 — six each in both the Master and Master Deluxe lineups. The two-door town sedans were the most popular by far with 95,050 built, but coupes were also good sellers. A total of 39,793 coupes like Thomas' rolled off Chevy assembly lines carrying base prices of $648, which was the lowest MSRP on the Chevy menu.

Thomas was determined to bring his Sweetie back to life. He started by fixing the starter and fuel pump, but then made a costly mistake when he started the car without cleaning out the old gas tank.

"I finally did get it started. It ran — it was a little rough — but it did run," he recalls. "Well, after I got done bouncing off the walls with excitement, I took a couple of pictures of it running, then I shut it off and went inside. The next day I went out to start it again, it just went [insert loud engine noise sounds]! Come to find out the fresh gas I had put in it had melted enough varnish and the varnish had gotten up into the engine and stuck the valves shut. Overnight it had crystallized right in the engine. I had to buy a whole new set of push rods and whole set of lifters … Now I preach that hard, hard: If you ever buy a car that hasn't started in a long time, before you start it, pull the tank on it and clean it all out. You'll save yourself a lot of problems."

The next big step in what Thomas termed "a rolling restoration" was to replace much of the interior "so it didn't smell like a bathroom," he said. "I drove it that way for a while and actually took it to some shows. It was all pretty much original, except for the interior.

"Most of the paint had popped off it. It had a lot of bare spots and lot of surface rust. I still had fun driving it and darn sure didn't have to worry about polishing it be-

The 1938 Chevrolet looks great today, and still carries its orignal inline six-cylinder engine.

fore went a show."

Thomas kept messaging the old '38 a little at a time, fixing a few body panels, then priming the back half of the car and re-chroming the rear bumper. "From the side it looked kind of funny," he said. "The back half looked good and front half was all original."

Thomas eventually primed the front half of the car, too, and got the rest of the chrome done. "It had aftermarket fender shirts on it so it looked like a low-rider. It really looked cool!" he said.

The finishing touch finally came in 2009 when the car got a shiny new suit of black paint. "I decided to bit the bullet," Thomas said. The car is now arguably better than new, with options like fender skirts, heater, defroster, clock and ashtray that were not in the car when it was ordered new.

After waiting all these years, Thomas has no problems putting some miles on his Chevy, often with his wife Peggy riding shotgun. "She loves it and loves to go for rides," Thomas said. The coupe's odometer now reads 54,000-plus miles, and Thomas has accounted for about 6,000 of those. The Chevy's days of sitting sedentary in a barn appear to be long gone.

"It runs fine, it just doesn't run real fast," Thomas joked. "It's the old babbit-beater engine. It's basically the old oil-splash system. It will run forever as long as you don't over-rap it.

"I get it out when the weather is good. I try to drive it at least once a week. I run across people who'll see the car and say, 'Hey, I remember when Mike's mom used to drive that car.' Some of the old-timers around here remember it."

GP IN THE NORTH WOODS

**Was that a rare Bantam jeep or something else trapped in the Wisconsin north woods?
Some military vehicles buffs had to find out.**

This story began in June 2001 when local Studebaker collector Cecil Scribner mentioned to military vehicle collector Buster Miller that he had spotted a "Bantam Jeep" in the woods behind the house of an elderly lady in northern Wisconsin. Scibner, who owns a septic systems business, had spotted the derelict vehicle when he had serviced the septic system at the woman's home.

Miller, who is a member of the Military Vehicle Preservation Group of Spooner couldn't resist such a tantalizing lead. Who knows what could be there? A proto-

This WWII era jeep clearly hadn't moved in many years.

type BRC? Scribner is not a jeep collector, so Miller had to wonder what had prompted him to say "Bantam?" Most folks who haven't been initiated in military jeep lore would have simply said they had spotted "an old World War II jeep," or "an old Army jeep." Scribner didn't use those terms, though, he specifically volunteered the name "Bantam." So, Miller went off to visit the old woman and her jeep, expecting the worst, but hoping for the best.

After exchanging pleasantries with the woman, Miller received permission to go back in the woods and look at the "old jeep." When he finally clawed his way through the covering foliage, Miller discovered that the vehicle was actually a 1941 Ford GP. What had prompted Scrib-

ner, the Studebaker collector, to call it a Bantam? A bit more exploring revealed the source of the label. Firmly seated in the dash was a set of Bantam-marked gauges.

Miller realized, even though it wasn't a Bantam, he still had one of those "right under your nose rare finds." He quickly shared the information with other members of military vehicle club to which he belonged. Kevin Kronlund and Thea De-Groot, members of the Spooner Military Vehicle Preservation Group (MVPG) decided to pay a visit the lady with the hopes of purchasing the vehicle. With seemingly little effort, the two parties determined a price and made the sale. The woman seemed only too happy to get rid of the rusty hulk. To her, there was nothing spe-

The source of the "Bantam" name for this discovery came from the gauges--So where is the Bantam from which these came?

cial about the old jeep.

The following weekend, armed with a M62 wrecker and flatbed trailer, Kronlund, Miller, and Ed Morgan drove to the cabin to "pluck the little gem from its resting place" (Buster's words). Safely loaded on the flatbed, the three carried the Jeep with Bantam gauges back to Kronlund's shop in Spooner. After some discussion, the Group decided to offer the jeep for sale, since the MVPG had just started their next project, a M28 Weasel.

This tale just goes to show that the "jeeps in the barns" (or in this case, "in the north woods of Wisconsin") are still there to be discovered. As you drive the countryside, keep looking deep into those treelines, abandoned barns, and piles of rusty metal. Who knows? Those Bantam gauges had to come from somewhere!

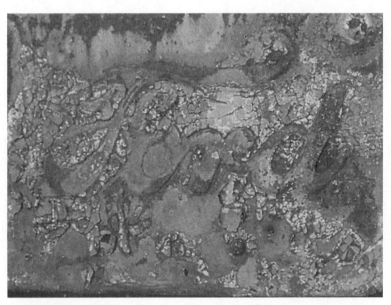

So it wasn't a Bantam ... a Ford script GP ain't so bad!

Story and photos by Brian Earnest

FAB '46

After years in a shed, this born-again
Ford Super Deluxe gets the royal treatment

John Lang had never restored a car before, but he took his time and transformed his battered old 1946 Ford into head-turning cream puff.

Sometimes in life, you just gotta take a chance.

There really is no other good explanation for why John Lang would want to stop at a stranger's house, knock on the door and inquire about an old Ford he heard might be sitting in a shed on the property.

Lang had never restored such a car. Never owned one, and never even owned a col-lector car before.

But "barn find" automobiles can have an irresistible appeal, and Lang, a resident of Marshfield, Wis., simply couldn't pass up the chance to drag an old car into the sun-light for the first time in years and give it a second chance in life.

"How long had it been sitting there? I couldn't tell you. A long time," said Lang

When the Ford was dragged out of a farm shed in 1998, it was mostly intact but in need of a total restoration. "It lasted through several wars, and it was pretty scarred up," Lang says.

of his beautiful 1946 Ford Super Deluxe coupe sedan. "It was sitting in a machine shed with a dirt floor, but it survived really well, I gotta say that.

"Another guy had told me about it and I decided to stop and see the [owner] and ask him about it. He said sure, he'd sell it."

"I tell everybody it had some scars on it. It lasted through several wars, and was definitely scarred up, but it wasn't in bad shape … I wanted it right away. Yup. My dad had a '47 Ford, and I liked flatheads, so I wanted to stick with a flathead from around this age

— 1946, '47, '48. I loaded 'er on a trailer and brought it home. And I got 'er running right away!"

That was back in 1998. A year later, Lang retired and began a three-year restoration that has turned the Ford into a real show-stopper. The deep-red coupe is now your quintessential Sunday fun machine, making regular appearances at local car shows and taking joy rides around central Wisconsin.

"I got it done in the spring of '02 and we just turned 10,000 miles on it," Lang

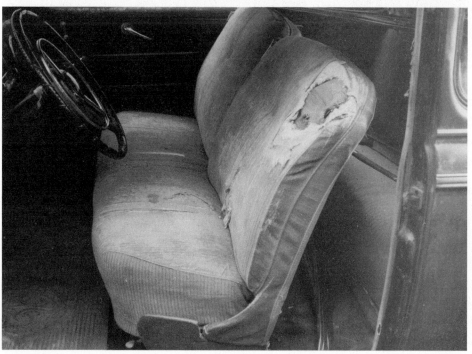

said. "That first year the speedometer didn't work, but we've got 10,000 miles on since that second year.

"I don't see many of them. Not many of them at all. Most of them are street-rodded. I put this one back to original, except for the paint. This car is mostly original, but most of these were rodded and chopped and had big engines put into them. I didn't do any of that."

The first postwar Fords are still extremely popular today, but they were positively red-hot when they first arrived in dealer showrooms in October of 1945. After four years with no new cars available, folks were lining up, literally, to get their hands on new automobiles, and Ford buyers were clamoring for new machines, even if the 1946s were only slightly updated versions of the 1942 offerings.

The front end was given a new grille that featured three horizontal chrome bars below a prominent set of Ford "wings" mounted to the bottom ends of the curved hood. Everything else on the car was virtually the same as in 1942, including the 225-cid six-cylinder or 239-cid flathead V-8, which were the only two engine choices in both of Ford's two tiers (Deluxe and Super Deluxe). The bottom-end Special that had been offered up until 1942 did not return after the war.

The top-end Super Deluxes featured twin sun visors, a horizontal chrome strip on the bodyside, bright trim around the windows, armrests on the doors, a horn ring and a few other minor upgrades. The Super Deluxes came in seven configurations: two-door coupe, two-door coupe sedan, two-door convertible, two- and four-door sedans, Sportsman "woodie" convertible, standard (steel) convertible and four-door station wagon.

The two-door sedan coupes like Lang's were second on the popularity charts that year among Fords. With a production total of 70,826, they were still well behind the two-door sedans, however; Ford built 163,370 of those.

The cars all rode on 114-inch wheelbases with overall lengths of 196.2 inches. The sedan coupes tipped the scales at 3,140 lbs. and carried a base sticker price of about $1,307.

All Fords carried a floor-shifted three-speed transmission and hydraulic drum brakes on all four 16-inch wheels. Brake hp for the flathead V-8 was rated at 100, with torque rated at 180 lbs.-ft.

Lang was able to save and restore almost everything on his Ford, including the engine and drive train. He did wind up buying a donor car, however, to help supply some missing trim pieces and a few other parts. "I was missing a some of the chrome on the trunk … I had it, but it was all bent up and beat up and the trunk didn't fit right. The seat — I don't know what they had in it for a seat, so the car that I bought had a seat that fit [right]. All the chrome is off the first one, except the chrome on the trunk. The second one I bought had the sun visor on it, so I took the sun visor off the second car and put it on this one.

"The drive train is all from the original car. We had everything completely rebuilt in it. It needed it!

Lang didn't really have a timetable for his Ford restoration, and the longer he worked on his car, the higher his standards seemed to get. He admits he didn't envision the car turning out this nice when he first dragged it home.

"No, I didn't, not when I started," he said. "But where do you quit, you know? You get into it and you don't know where to stop, so you just keep going.

"I knew it would be a job, but I knew it wasn't in the worst shape. The floor was good in it, and they've fixed a lot worse ones than this."

The shiny burgundy paint is clearly an upgrade over the original Royal Maroon offered by Ford in 1946. In perhaps his biggest concession to non-originality, Lang extended the deep red to the interior, where he used red to replace the navy blue that had originally been part of the blue-and-gray cockpit color scheme — including the steering wheel. The Ford still carries its red-on-black instruments, radio and dash brightwork. "It's close to the original color, but it's brighter and more modern," Lang said.

"The older ones had a duller enamel with a duller finish. We went with burgundy ... I think we hit it just right."

The interior was re-upholstered in its original gray, but the seat fabric now has some red striping to match the deep red paint inside and out.

Even though he put three-plus years of time, effort and expense into the Ford, Lang made sure he didn't turn out a trailer queen. His goal was to have beautiful, dependable toy that he could show off, and the '46 has turned into exactly that.

"It was my first one and probably my last one," he said. "I don't have the ambition to do another one. I'm going to enjoy this one for a while yet."

Story and photos by Dr. Roger Leir

DERHAM DODGE DREAM REALIZED

Reviving a one-off custom 1948 Dodge coupe

Derham Body Co. is believed to have built only one of these 1948 Dodge coupes with a Studebaker-style wrap-around rear window. The car was found in Vermont in 1985 in tough shape.

The name of the Derham Body Co. of Rosemont, Pa., rings a familiar bell for those of us who are avid car collectors. Even some with a casual interest will recall seeing cars bodied by this famous auto body manufacturer. Among companies that bodied automobiles starting in the early 1900s, Derham stood with the best, working its styling touches on vehicles until the late 1960s.

As time marched forth from the company's founding, so did the desire for custom-bodied automobiles. Derham produced many coachbuilt bodies through the 1930s and also managed to stay active through World War II for two main reasons: The company was able to skillfully transform automakers' factory bodies into custom-designed works of art, and it had a dealer contract with Chrysler Corp.

For many years, Derham seemed to have flourished under the great wing of Chrysler, even prior to the dealer arrangement. After World War II ended, Derham tailored its interest to building series custom cars to attract the public to purchase Chrysler Corp. automobiles. Essentially, it built custom cars for showroom display.

In 1948, Derham built two custom polo wagons at the request of New York Dodge dealer C.M. Bishop. Industrial designer Donald Diskey and Enos Derham were believed to have been responsible for the engineering and design of the Dodge Derhams. Chrysler archives contain photos of one of the Derham-bodied polo wagons, but the actual vehicles faded into obscurity and were never heard of or seen again. The archive also includes photos of a Derham-bodied 1948 Dodge coupe.

Unlike the polo wagons, the 1948 Custom Derham coupe survived. This car is believed to be Derham's own design and was taken from dealer showroom to showroom for display purposes only in order to attract public attention. Records show there was no intention by Chrysler to mass-produce this automobile, although some will argue that there was talk of producing a line of custom-series Dodges.

There were already two Dodge coupes in the 1948 lineup, yet Derham created this third style to add additional passenger space in the rear seat area.

The car's interior included a chrome ring on the steering wheel, seven-button Philco radio, electric clock, two-speed wiper control and a passenger side heater with defroster.

This very rare automobile is totally unique in its appearance and design. It was born as a five-window club coupe. Derham removed the original top, shortened the package tray, and moved the rear seat backward about 4 inches, giving more leg room in the rear compartment. Derham also designed and installed a wrap-around rear window, similar to 1947-and-later Studebaker coupes of the era. The window design is similar in appearance, but in many ways, it is totally different from these Studebakers.

Other Derham modifications included a totally different interior design, dual interior lamps, custom rearview mirror, upholstered trunk that included a Derham-badged tool kit case and custom-designed Derham hubcaps. All of the trim from the beltline upward is of Derham design. The coachbuilder did use a stock seven-button MoPar radio made by Philco, an electric clock, two-speed electric windshield wipers, a passenger-side heater unit with defroster, backup light, interior deck lid light, passenger-side tissue holder and the usual "Derham" script

This very rare automobile is totally unique in its appearance and design. It was born as a five-window club coupe.

badges. The drive train is stock 1948 Dodge with Fluid Drive.

After these 1948 Dodges were bodied by Derham, it appears the company concentrated on modifying production bodies of Chryslers, Cadillacs, Packards and Lincolns. Derham sales catalogs show that, in 1967, the company was still completing custom modifications, but mainly to Lincolns and Cadillacs, having totally given up its franchise arrangements with Chrysler some years earlier.

This one-off Derham-bodied Dodge coupe was first sold privately to Gertrude Fisher of Brooklyn, N.Y., in January 1950. In April 1985, the Joseph Leir Memorial Auto Collection of Moorpark, Calif., purchased it. There is no information available for the 35 missing years between 1950 and 1985.

My father, Joseph Leir, was a devout admirer of Dodge automobiles and owned the auto collection. The mainstay of the collection was its entire series of Dodge models built between 1942 and 1948. It consisted of 110 cars in various stages of restoration as well as parts cars and show automobiles. As collection manager, I was responsible for housing, maintaining and overseeing

the restoration of the cars.

One of my other duties was the procurement of additions to the collection. In early 1985, I was told about this one-off 1948 Dodge Derham coupe and located it in Vermont. I was told that the automobile had been stored outside in the severe northeastern weather for many years and deteriorated to "basket case" condition. I contacted the owner and he forwarded photos. What I heard about the condition of the car seemed to be accurate. Much of the car had rusted through and pieces were hanging on by a thread. A deal was then struck with the owner and arrangements were made to ship the car by open carrier to Moorpark.

When the car arrived, a small crowd had gathered outside of the main entrance to our museum. Most of the individuals, neighbors and collectors all found it amusing that this "thing" was being delivered. The very act of unloading the car brought further damage and the loss of rusted metal, which literally fell to the pavement. I could only guess how much rust was lost during its trip to California.

Strangely enough, the car was on all four tires and wheels and rolled with ease. We pushed the vehicle into the shop area where

Derham created an interior unique to the Dodge and enough original upholstery remained so it could be accurately restored.

Freddie, my shop foreman, stood trying to figure out a plan of attack. We instantly knew that of all the restorations, this was going to be the most difficult. It was decided to strip the body from the frame, leaving the running gear intact. It took about a month to accomplish this task. On a Friday evening, I received a call from Freddie asking if I could stop by the shop for a surprise. When I arrived, I noticed he had the Derham body sitting outside the shop and that there was a chassis complete with engine and steering wheel sitting in the shop area. I soon found that this was the Derham Dodge's chassis and drive train. My next surprise was that he started the engine, idled it down to a whisper-smooth purr and then grinned at me with a look of satisfaction.

I wish I had the ability to predict the future from that moment on as many sets of dire circumstances occurred in short order, including the death of my father, Freddie's death and my own massive heart attack. The collection had to be sold and the only vehicle preserved was the Derham Dodge coupe.

It took all of the 24 years between 1985 and 2009 to finish restoring the automobile. Many of the parts specifically made by Derham had to be remanufactured, most by the hands of skilled artisans. We were also the recipients of some good fortune. There was enough of the original upholstery material left to obtain new-old-stock material and have most of the interior redone. All of the newly upholstered pieces were sealed in plastic and placed in closed-environment storage for safekeeping. There was also enough of the padded top material to have a duplicate top made when the time came to re-install it. Another piece of good fortune came when the color Derham had painted the car was still present underneath the deteriorating top material, making it easier to duplicate the color scheme.

Finally, the Derham was completed in October 2009 and was shown at a meet by the Western Region of the Antique Automobile Club of America in La Quinta, Calif., where it won its First Junior award. In addition, the car was recently shown at another Western Regional AACA meet where it won a First Senior award.

Story and photos by John Gunnell

BABIED BUICK

Even the battery is original on this 20,000-mile 1951

This 1951 Buick has sat for years — lifting the side-opening hood left handprints in the dust. The original owner parked the car on boards to allow for better circulation and rust prevention.

This is the story of a true "Rip Van Winkle" car — a fabulous 1951 Buick that was lovingly preserved by its original owner, in almost new condition, for 59 years. When examined by *Old Cars Weekly* after its owner recently passed away, it was found stored in a simple garage in a small city less than 20 miles from *OCW*'s Iola, Wis. headquarters. It is truly a car that "slept" more than Washington Irving's fictional protagonist who snoozed for two decades, a fact that can be verified by the *OCW* staff.

The Buick Special Deluxe two-door hardtop is Buick Model No. 51-45R, Body Style No. 51-4337, and its odometer reads just 20,391 miles. Former *Old Cars Weekly Price Guide* editor Ken Buttolph, who is renowned for his love of well-kept cars (especially Buicks), recalls that he first saw this one in 1955 and says that, even then, it stood out as a "babied" Buick. Amazingly, it has always been kept in an unheated, unlit wooden garage and is still sitting on its factory-original tires.

Walter Zemple purchased this amazing car on May 25, 1951, from Waupaca Motor Sales in Waupaca, Wis. Like many Buicks of its era, this one is finished in black lacquer paint (applied by the factory) and has a two-tone gray interior. The seats of this example have been covered with blankets and sheets, which has helped them remain perfect. Likewise, the floor mats, door panels, headliner, package shelf and trunk trim are all as new, and the glove box still holds a key slug sticker and an instruction sticker for the tire pressure, jacking, engine oil and transmission oil.

The inside of the car's wheel wells still have factory black paint, although there is some minor surface rust. The chassis and other under-body parts have a light coat of storage rust. Meanwhile, the front suspension looks well lubricated. The front badge still has its blue-and-red coloring.

This special Buick Special's combination trunk badge and handle is faded red with some very minor lifting of the red. All of the chrome and stainless trim is in very nice to excellent condition, with only the lightest crazing on some pieces, probably due to its Korean War-era plating. The bumper jack is in the trunk and looks new.

Under the hood looks good and appears to retain a factory "X" chalk mark. The car's straight-eight engine has original color paint on the rocker arm cover, and the car has an add-on, canister-type oil filter assembly that is a correct aftermarket item for its era. This may have been dealer installed, but it is not listed on the car's original bill of sale.

The Buick has the standard three-speed manual synchromesh transmission, and the 7.60 x 15 black-sidewall U.S. Royal Air Ride tires still hold air after nearly 60 years.

Other factory options on the bill of sale include a heater, a radio and antenna, back-up lamps, a Buick Flex steering wheel, Foam

The seats of this example have been covered with blankets and sheets, which has helped them remain perfect. Likewise, the floor mats, door panels, headliner, package shelf and trunk trim are all as new.

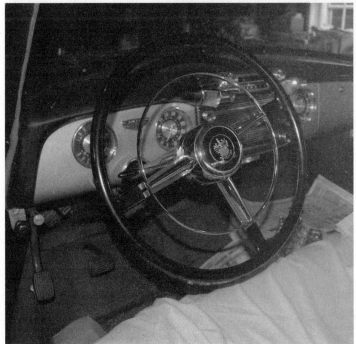

Heavy blankets and sheets protected the cloth seats extremely well on this pristine survivor. The steering wheel and dashboard look brand new.

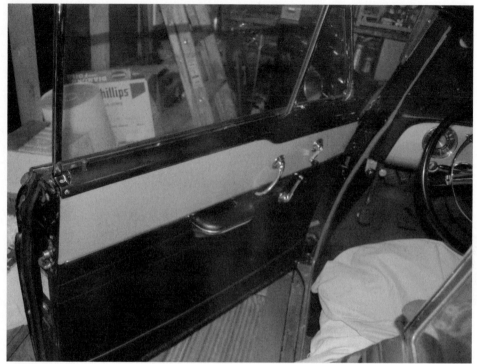

The last time original door panels looked this good was in a 1951 Buick showroom.

Tex (foam rubber) seat cushions, directional signals, an accessory group, a spare tire and tube. The car also has an exhaust deflector with the square Buick logo.

When it was new, this "three porthole" Buick Special featured sweepspear body-side moldings and style-side trim that gave it and other Special Deluxe models an upscale look. (All two-door hardtop Special Rivieras such as this car had the Deluxe trim.) All Specials grew in length and had soft-cushioned rear seats with more than 63 in. of hip room. The "Special" name appeared on the deck lid, and prices started at

$1,917 for the Riviera.

1951 Buicks rode on rugged, X-braced chassis with a relatively low center of gravity. They used a rigid torque-tube drive system. The Buick salesman's guide stated, "The major source of Buick's swayless, swerve-free ever-level stability comes from its solid and sure-footed chassis, giving the car road poise and a solid 'seat' on the highway."

A new "Push-Bar" front end was seen in 1951. The 25 small, stamped-steel grille bars did not cover the bumper as in 1950 and were designed to "give" with

the massive wraparound bumper. Blade-style bumper guards added to front-end protection.

The 1951 Buick look was promoted as "Dreamline Styling" and featured tapered, car-length fenders that blended into the main body line. A colorful ad promoted the 1951 Buick Special as "Room With Zoom." Buick's volume-production line was the center of attention this year, and its cars sold well.

With this car's 263.3-cid straight-eight and manual-transmission combination, horsepower was rated at 120 units at 3,600

rpm and 215 lbs.-ft. of torque. The engine had five main bearings and hydraulic-valve lifters with a two-barrel carburetor.

The Riviera coupe in the Special series was offered only in the Buick Special Deluxe line (Series 40D). These models had plusher interiors, full-length body-side moldings, bright window outlines, rear window moldings and "Special" scripts on the front fenders, just behind the wheel openings and above the tip of the side spear.

Any old-car hobbyist would be impressed by Zemple's preservation efforts of his Series 40D Special Deluxe Riviera

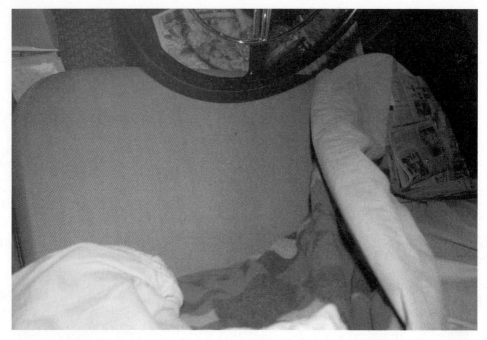

Heavy blankets had been used to perfectly preserve the Buick's upholstery.

coupe. The car was even found perched on boards to allow better circulation of air beneath the car, thus reducing rust-causing moisture.

In the trunk and in the rear passenger compartment are NOS parts to allow the car to be properly maintained throughout its life. Zemple had other cars as well, including a 1951 Buick Special Riviera coupe to serve as a parts car for this one. However, there is no indication he ever used a part from it on his pristine car.

The well-preserved Buick is now in the possession of Mr. Zemple's heirs, who are aware of its "special" nature and have a good idea of its relative value in today's marketplace. They are taking care to keep the car all-original throughout.

Before time had made it the exceedingly remarkable car it is today, Zemple displayed his well-preserved Buick in the Iola Old Car Show. He's passed away now, but perhaps his Special will someday make another appearance.

Story and photos by Angelo Van Bogart

BACK FROM THE BRINK

It took more than 30 years to take a 1955 Plymouth Belvedere from the salvage yard to the show field

Compared to the 1954 models, Plymouths were downright wild with the "Forward Look" in 1955. This car has had its own wild ride, going back at least to the period it was pulled from an Oglivie, Minn., salvage yard in 1975.

Not many souls under the guillotine get a reprieve, but this 1955 Plymouth was rescued more than once from a grim future.

"This car has been rescued from a junk yard twice," said Howard Cassidy, the brave soul who rescued the featured 1955 Plymouth Belvedere convertible from a salvage yard east of Ogilvie, Minn., in 1975 when he was 21 years old.

"I accidentally stumbled on it when I was looking for parts for something else," the Forest Lake, Minn., resident said. "Recognizing what it was, I was kind of intrigued by it."

The car had last been registered in 1964, according to the license plates it wore, and Cassidy pictured it on the road again.

That summer, 35 years ago, he pulled the rare black-and-white Belvedere, one of just 8,473 convertibles built that year, from the salvage yard — for the first time.

"The yard owner had to cut a tree off of it," Cassidy said. "Quite a large tree had fallen on it. He also had to move six or eight cars to get it out. It was pretty badly buried in the yard." Other trees also had to be removed, and for all that labor, the yard owner wasn't asking for much.

"He said, 'If it's worth taking out of here, it has to be worth $50,'" Cassidy said. He quickly agreed to that price, which turned out to be a bigger bargain than he expected after all the trees and cars were moved. "He really worked for that $50," Cassidy added.

However, Cassidy didn't get a show car for that $50 — the Plymouth was a project, if not less, in every sense of the word. "When you opened up the trunk, there was nothing in there but the frame and the gas tank," Cassidy said. "The rocker panels were gone, the quarter panels were gone, the fronts of the front fenders were gone."

In addition, the tree that had fallen on the car broke some of the car's top bows. Mechanically, the car was rough, too.

"The engine was stuck, the oil pan was in the trunk on the gas tank," Cassidy said. "One of the cylinders was rusted from top to bottom. I think they had blown a head gasket and someone was trying to save it.

"The sad part was, the owner told me it was in really nice shape when it arrived in the yard. It really was complete; the only thing I can think of that was missing is the spare tire. When we pulled it out of the yard, you could see the imprint of where the mufflers were. There were brown spots of where they were, but they were gone... rusted away."

Although the '55 Belvedere convertible wasn't the first car Cassidy saved from a salvage yard; he had retrieved a 1941 Plymouth truck from nearby Ogilvie Iron earlier — but retrieving the convertible was probably the act that made Cassidy's father think he was the craziest.

"My father thought I was out of my mind," Cassidy said. Soon after, however, Cassidy's father joined the "crazy train" and took steps to help him save the car, including rescuing it from its second stint in the salvage yard.

"When I moved to Tucson, Ariz. [from Minnesota], I was not able to take all my cars with," Cassidy said. "Since I didn't

The car had last been registered in 1964, according to the license plates it wore, and Cassidy pictured it on the road again.

Fins were fully — but subtly — incorporated into the Plymouth sheet metal for 1955. The instrument panel is symmetrical with the radio and glove box front and center. During this car's restoration, the interior was completely reupholstered.

The rear of the Sport Coupe as it arrived at Cassidy's home.

have much in the '55, I decided to leave it behind. I went and asked the man I purchased the car from if I could put the car back in the junk yard until I could come back and get it. He said, 'No problem.' So I took the car back to the junk yard and parked it in an area where not too many people were allowed."

The convertible sat in the yard for two more years until Cassidy's parents, who had also moved to Arizona, offered to bring it back to Arizona with them during a vacation to Minnesota.

While in Arizona during the early 1980s, Cassidy's father located a much more solid and relatively decent Belvedere Sport Coupe in a salvage yard. Unfortunately, the yard owner would not allow Cassidy to buy

the car whole as Cassidy had done earlier with the convertible. Regardless, he found a way to get the parts he needed.

"My dad found it in the junk yard and told me about it," Cassidy said. "For some reason, the yard owner didn't want me to buy the whole car, but he would sell me the back end. When I got there, he had the body off the frame and was ready for me to start cutting. He had the roof cut off and he even supplied the torch. I cut it down the middle, in front of the posts behind the doors."

Before he went to the salvage yard, Cassidy wanted to make sure it would be worth cutting up the hardtop, so he began some prep work on the convertible.

"I figured I would cut the convertible first, and if I messed it up, I would just junk

it," he said. Fortunately, the convertible wasn't irreversibly damaged and the work continued.

"I was thrilled to find that coupe in Tucson, and even then, it was a little rusty," Cassidy said. "I put in the lower quarters and the trunk floor and the rear pan [from the Sport Coupe] in one piece so I had my dad and a neighbor help me hulk that into the convertible. I have a photo of my dad with his head cocked and looking at it thinking, 'What a mess!'"

Eventually, Cassidy made his way north to Minnesota again. Work had been stalled on the convertible since the mid-1980s, but in 2005, Cassidy gained more work space and felt compelled to begin work on the car.

"I told my wife, 'If we don't do something with it soon, we might as well get rid of it,'" Cassidy said. "At that time, it was time to get serious."

Although Cassidy had already proven his automotive talents with the Plymouth — in addition to swapping rear body sections, he had actually gotten the car running and driving with a different engine — he needed professionals with more experience to complete it.

"The body was still so bad, I just couldn't

finish it — it was beyond me," he said. "In 2005, I let Jack Schultz in Medford, Minn., take over. He had a rotisserie. He took the body off the frame and rebuilt the body and did the frame. He's the one that got it as beautiful as it is now."

Howard Boyd in Mankato, Minn., completed the top and interior, and Cassidy dug into other aspects of the restoration.

"I did the engine and the transmission," he said. He also spent a summer polishing and removing dents from the seemingly miles of stainless Belvedere trim that wraps around the sides of the top-of-the-line Plymouth. Around the trim, Cassidy decided to change the color from its original black-and-white to a red-and-white combination.

"There was one in Tucson I ran into in a transmission shop and it was painted the same color as mine and that's what made me paint it red and white," Cassidy said. Also, "My Dad's favorite color was red. That helped decide the color, too."

Unfortunately, Cassidy's father didn't live to see the Plymouth hit the road again in 2006, and Howard himself even questioned whether he'd see it barrel down a stretch of two-lane.

"I can't even believe it sometimes that I have been able to drive this thing before I die," Cassidy said. "I just wish my dad had lived to ride in it. He had commented he wanted to go for a ride in it and he didn't."

The Cassidy family isn't alone in its shock to see the Plymouth driving again. Other Plymouth Owner's Club members have shared their disbelief that Cassidy's 1955 Belvedere convertible went from a junkyard dog to a show queen.

"People are astonished that it's on the road," Cassidy said. He added that 1955 Plymouths aren't a common sight, a point other hobbyist frequently acknowledge.

"One year, at [the Iola Old Car Show], two guys walked up to the car and said, 'When was the last time you saw a 1955 Plymouth, much less a convertible?'"

Although Cassidy has an eye for the rare and unusual, he's sure his days of pulling cars out of salvage yards are over.

"I don't know if I would again," he said. "I bought two cars in boxes — my restored '39 Plymouth coupe was all in boxes and [my project] Terraplane was, too. I don't always have the energy to work on the Terraplane, and that was all there."

If the right car popped up in a salvage yard or a field, we'll bet it would be tough for Cassidy to turn down the chance to save it. He's already spotted a bullet-nose Studebaker business coupe in a Delano, Minn., salvage yard that's caught his eye. When asked if he'd consider restoring it, he works hard to make his reply sound convincing.

"Oh, it's too rough, it's too rough."

Maybe it is, but that's never stopped this salvage yard saint before.

By Harold Drake

SAVED FROM THE CRUSHER

Good fortune rescues convertible from the end of the road

The author's 1956 Bel Air after its restoration.

Around 1980, I was running an errand across town when I spotted a 1956 Chevrolet Bel Air convertible in an auto repair shop. It was a daily driver in need of restoration. I stopped and asked if it was for sale, but it was not and my heart sank.

I learned it was in the mechanic's shop for a broken shift lever housing on the column. I had the part the owner needed, so I went home to fetch the part for the car. I figured if I couldn't buy the Chevy, I would get the satisfaction of helping keep it on the road. But this was not the end of the story.

Two months later, I went to my favorite wrecking yard in Gardena, Calif., and there was the same Bel Air convertible. Only this time, it was on a forklift headed for the crusher pile! I got the fork lift operator's attention and made him stop in his tracks. He took the car back to the office where I purchased it for $200.

I found out the '56 Chevy had been stolen and vandalized since I had first seen it. The glass was broken and the ignition was popped out. I had it towed home, got it running and drove it around until I restored it.

Mechanically, the car was perfect. The engine, transmission, brakes, etc., were in fine condition. I removed the front end and undertook a firewall-forward restoration. With the front end off, I completed the body and paint work and gave it a new interior.

I am glad I saved this car from the crusher, and to this day, I still can't believe that I went to this wrecking yard at the exact moment that the 1956 Chevrolet was on its way to the crusher. I sold it years ago, but I am sure someone out there is enjoying it.

The Bel Air was moments from becoming scrap metal.

A LONG WAY HOME

Former garage companions wind up together again thanks to Minnesota man

Randy Guyer's love for "Letter Car" Chryslers started with this
1960 300-F convertible.

*O*ld Cars Weekly reader Randy Guyer of Minnesota fell out of the old car hobby as he concentrated on work and family. He jumped back in full-bore when he made an impulse bid on a finned 1958 Dodge Regal Lancer at a 2007 Barrett-Jackson auction. Since then, he's been hot for Chrysler 300 "Letter Cars," especially black models. Since 2007, he's added a 1957 Chrysler 300-C hardtop and a special 300-F convertible to his collection, each following his

"the blacker the better" mantra.

Guyer's newfound affinity for ebony Chrysler 300s has been shared by collectors on the East Coast and in Texas. In fact, he can say he's shared titles with one of these collectors, because his 1957 and 1960 Chrysler 300s have shared garage space at least twice as these cars skipped across the country since the 1960s, leapfrogging one another from Connecticut to Texas before rejoining in Minnesota.

Built only as coupes starting in 1955 and as convertibles from 1957 to 1965, the "Letter Cars" were supposed to offer performance to the executive class.

The following is the story of these star-crossed Chrysler 300s in Guyer's words.

1960 Chrysler 300-F convertible

This rare Chrysler was the last 300-F convertible produced for the 1960 model year. After Chrysler made four more 300-F coupes, 300-F production ended to make way for the 1961 300-G models. Built only as coupes starting in 1955 and as convertibles from 1957 to 1965, the "Letter Cars" were supposed to offer performance to the executive class. The competition grew to include such automobiles as the Ford Thunderbird and Buick Riviera in the sports/luxury class. Only 248 convertibles and 964 coupes in the 300 series were built for the 1960 model year.

This final 300-F was built June 7, 1960, and was shipped on July 5 to Plaza Motors, Inc. in New Haven, Conn., where Wallace Lines of Milford, Conn., was awaiting delivery of this special custom-ordered vehicle. This car may have been the most highly optioned 300-F convertible produced that year. Two of the rarest options on this car are

its power vacuum door locks and two-zone air conditioning. Other options include six-way power seats, power antenna, remote control outside mirror, Golden Touch radio and tinted glass.

The Chrysler's body type is No. 845, the designation for a Chrysler 300-F convertible, with a BB-1 paint code for Formal Black. Its trim code is No. 353 for beige leather. The engine is the standard Chrysler 300-F powerplant — the 413-cid "wedge head" V-8 with dual long-ram intake manifolds, each hoisting a four-barrel carburetor. This performance package provided 375 hp. The transmission is the standard push-button, three-speed TorqueFlite automatic.

In December 1965, Lines sold the 300-F convertible to Harry DeSiena of nearby Stratford, just one town away. DeSiena was an early finned car collector who appreciated the styling, beauty, luxury, power and performance of these cars, often referred to as "beautiful brutes." His enthusiasm led DeSiena and his eldest son Tommy to collect cars to the point of near bankruptcy. Stashed away in garages and sheds near his

The 300-F is pictured here before it began its comprehensive restoration. This 300-F is the last "Letter Car" convertible built for 1960.

Guyer's 1957 Chrysler 300-C hardtop shared a Connecticut owner with his 300-F convertible from the 1960s until the early 2000s. Unlike the 300-F convertible, this 300-C hardtop has relatively few options.

home, DiSiena's collection would stay hidden away for 40 years. All the while, there had been rumors circulating around Connecticut of this car's existence. No one knew for sure that it was still there, because it had been decades since anyone had last seen it.

The 300-F had become a bit of a legend — a faint and distant memory.

In 2001, DeSiena died and his son, Tommy, assumed custody of the car collection. When Tommy's health began to fail in 2003, he started selling some of the cars. He began with some of the least rare and collectible ones while hanging onto the most precious ones as long as possible. Tommy died in 2005.

In 2006, DeSiena's youngest son, Richard "Rick" DiSiena, took charge of the estate and continued selling the collection. Eventually, Rick pulled the 300-F convertible from the shed and sold it to a local automobile broker, who immediately sold the car to a Mr. Schibley, another car collector in Texas.

In May 2007, after owning the car for less than one year, Schibley tried to sell the car at auction in Houston. The auction company had a projected sell price of $125,000-150,000, but the car did not sell.

Later in 2007, Schibley sold the car to Andy Bernbaum, a MoPar parts dealer and car collector of note in Boston, Mass. Bernbaum planned to restore it at some point.

In June of 2008, I had a phone conversation with Jerry Kopecky, a car restorer in Iola, Wis. I told Kopecky that if he ever ran across one of these "banker's hot rods" that was for sale, I might be interested. Furthermore, I wanted an original black car with lots of options, including air conditioning. Since there were only 248 built 50 years ago and only 60 or so are known to exist today, I imagine my wishes made Kopecky chuckle on the inside. However, about two weeks later, Kopecky called me to say Bernbaum's black 300-F convertible was available in Boston.

We were invited to see the car in person, and so off we went in early July. The car ran rough, was very complete and the metal was in relatively rust-free condition. It was clear the car was unrestored and very original, except for one repaint many years ago.

In a nod to its originality, the original "Blue Streak" spare tire is still in the car's trunk, and while it has been used, it still holds air. The car also retains its AstraDome gauge cluster with a speedometer that goes up to 150 mph for a reason — it has 375 hp on tap! The AstraDome gauge cluster is a space-age-looking unit that gives off a beautiful glow to reduce eye strain and glare at night, due to its electro-luminescent illumination. On the inside, this Chrysler is pure early-'60s.

After striking a deal with Bernbaum for its purchase, I took delivery of this 300-F convertible, the last one built, in August 2008. Along with it came an old title dating back to December 1965, when Lines sold the car to DeSiena.

1957 Chrysler 300-C coupe

The 300-C was the fastest and most powerful American production automobile for '57.

The 300-C in this story was built on May 20, 1957, and shipped to A. Coppola Motor Sales of New Haven, Conn. It is one of 1,767 coupes and 484 convertibles produced that model year.

The body type is No. 566 for a Chrysler

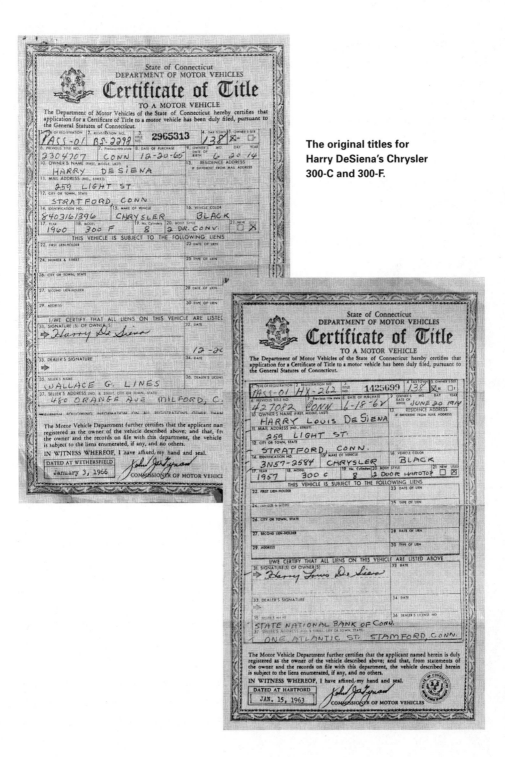

The original titles for Harry DeSiena's Chrysler 300-C and 300-F.

300-C coupe with paint code A for Jet Black and trim code 60 for beige leather trim. The engine is the 392-cid Hemi V-8 with dual quads providing 375 hp and backed by a three-speed, push-button TorqueFlite automatic.

Factory options on this car include power steering, Music Master Radio, heater and Solex (tinted) glass. Dealer A. Coppola Motor Sales installed the 48-spoke Chrysler wire wheels before the buyer took delivery.

In January 2010, a friend called to tell me that he saw an ad for a 300-C offered for sale in Celina, Texas. He knew that I collected late-'50s and early-'60s finned cars and that I would perhaps be interested in the car. I ended up buying the unrestored 48,000-mile original black 300-C sight unseen over the phone a couple days later from Ryan Poulos of Celina. The 300-C was a good, rust-free car that was complete, but it was not running. These cars are among the most desirable "Letter Cars" that Chrysler ever built, though, so I felt it was a good find.

It wasn't until I agreed to purchase the car from Poulos that I learned the 300-C came with a title showing the DiSiena family had owned it since the 1960s. In fact, it had been owned by the same collectors for four decades, and those collectors had owned my 300-F convertible from 1965 to the 2000s.

The 300-C's Connecticut title dated to June 1962 when Harry DiSiena bought the car from the State National Bank of Stamford, Conn. I do not know why the bank owned the car, nor do I know the car's ownership history from 1957 until 1962. However, much of the car's subsequent history is well known.

I learned that in March 2009, Poulos found the 300-C offered for sale by Richard "Rick" DeSiena in Stratford, Conn. Poulos called DiSiena and worked out a deal to purchase the car. Poulos found the 300-C inside a dilapidated shed where it had been sitting since 1969 when it was last driven. Like the 300-F convertible, the 300-C had been owned by Harry DiSiena, Rick's father, and had been driven in the early 1960s by Tommy DiSiena, Rick's bother.

The 300-C was dirty but relatively unscathed after slumbering in the Connecticut garage for 40 years. It's possible that my 300-F convertible had sat right next to the 300-C all those years until they met the same fate — joining my car collection.

I also found out that, in 1964, Tommy DiSienna took Rick to the New York World's Fair in this car, and Rick (then 8 years old) stuck a souvenir world's fair sticker on the rear window, where it remains. It became one of the last cars to be sold from the DiSiena estate, probably for sentimental reasons.

Restoring the 1960 300-F

The restoration goal is to put the 300-F convertible back to the same or better condition than it left the factory. It was too far gone to avoid restoration, and so the work began in January 2009 at Kopecky's Klassics. The odometer read 83,922 miles and remained at that setting through restoration. Due to the rarity, uniqueness and provenance of this car, Kopecky and I agreed that it deserves a complete body-off-frame, every-nut-and-bolt rotisserie restoration. I want the highest-quality car that we can achieve in regards to craftsmanship and authenticity.

We anticipate the restoration to be complete in 2012, thus taking 3-1/2 years. This is typical for a car such as this, with its complex mechanical systems and hard-to-find parts. Nevertheless, these old cars are a perfect timeline of American history that should be preserved and displayed.

Refreshing the 1957 300-C

The first order of business in restoring this car was to get it running. Once we proved that the engine would run, and the transmission and brakes worked, we could then determine what to do with the body and interior.

Since much of an old car's value comes from retaining its original engine and drive train, we needed to be cautious not to ruin anything. It was not as simple as we thought to get it running. Everything seemed to be in place to make it run, but it refused. After a lot of head scratching, we discovered that under the dash, Tommy DiSiena had wired a pair of red lamps to the ignition wire when he was a teenager. These lamps were supposed to turn on when the car was running and make a cool red glow into the car's interior. Surely, the chicks would dig that! Unfortunately, the lamps put too much current draw on the ignition wire and it became hot, melted the insulation and shorted out on the dash. Then the car wouldn't run, so into the shed it went. I am sure Tommy figured he would get it going again someday, but as often happens, life got in the way, and it sat for the next 40 years with the rest of the collection.

Although the car was running in the summer of 2010, I decided to have Kopecky pull the engine and transmission in the winter of 2010-2011 and completely rebuild them. We also decided to install new exhaust, brakes, gas tank, re-chromed bumpers and new wheels and tires. To get the car into safe driving condition, all of the lamps underwent repair as necessary. Body and interior restoration will commence in the next few years.

While the 300-F convertible is highly optioned for a car if its kind and time, this '57 300-C has very few options. It is a very basic, high-end car. It makes a person wonder why someone would order such an expensive car without the creature comforts of air-conditioning, power seats and windows and the like. Being the fastest production car in America in 1957, perhaps the original owner intended to go racing.

By Angelo Van Bogart
Photos from Mid America Motorworks

A BARN GOOD 'VETTE

Mike and Blake Yager uncover hidden 1957 Corvette ... and leave it untouched!

Blake (left) and Mike Yager (right) of Mid America Motorworks pose with the 1957 Corvette they recently unearthed from a barn just 40 miles from their business' corporate headquarters in Effingham, Ill. According to Mike Yager, the Corvette had been parked for 35-40 years and, "needless to say, this thing has had possums sleep in it."

Those who dabble in cars occasionally get leads on interesting cars for sale. Those who eat, sleep and breathe cars in business and pleasure get barraged with them. Mike Yager, "head cheerleader" for the largest outfitter of Corvette parts, re-

pairs and upgrades, falls under the latter category.

"Pretty regularly, people say 'I have a Corvette for sale,'" said Yager of Mid America Motorworks in Effingham, Ill. "The older it is, the more you hold on to your chair for the price — most are not very reasonable."

Even though Yager receives tons of tips, most of them don't pan out. But a lead Yager received last summer grabbed his attention.

"A guy stopped by my office a few days before the Fourth of July and said he had a Corvette for sale," Yager recalled. "I asked how long he had it and he said, '35-40 years.'"

About that time, Yager's ears perked up and he grabbed on to his chair as he prepared to ask the "big" question — how much?

"I said, 'What are you asking for the car?' and he said, 'I have been looking at the prices of these cars and I know what they're worth.' Then he quoted me a price and it was reasonable," Yager said.

The thought of a straight-axle Corvette was appealing, but the idea of hunting down a true "barn find" Corvette was irresistible. Yager knew he had to jump on the Corvette — a desirable 1957 model — lest he lose out on the opportunity. When he asked about looking at the car the next day, the car's owner said it wasn't possible. It would have to be that day.

To share in the rare experience, Yager called on his son, Blake, the corporate director for Mid America Motorworks and a Corvette enthusiast himself. This would not be the first time Blake had bought a Corvette with his dad, but it was one of the first times he had 100 percent approval from his father.

"Well, the first car that I bought 'with my father's guidance' was our blue 1964 [Corvette] Styling Car," Blake recalled. "My brother and I decided we *had* to get this car for my dad for Father's Day a few years back. We helped him bid on the car and even let him write the check for it in the end!"

This experience would be different. Together, the duo hopped in their car and made the 40-mile trek to examine the mysterious Corvette. The Yagers soon realized they were about to uncover a car so well-hidden, Louis and Clark would have walked right by it.

"We pulled up in the country and the weeds were growing up 3-4 feet tall and I said, 'Where's the car?'" the elder Yager recalled. "You could see an old house about 250-300 feet in the woods, then two barns came into view."

Traversing through tall grass and brush wasn't half as challenging as opening the barn door where the Corvette was said to be stored.

"The door was nailed shut, so we found the pry bar and it moved 2 feet and it hit a tree," Yager said. "A tree had grown up and the door wouldn't open. On the ground was an old rusty saw and we picked up that saw and started sawing on the tree. Finally, the saw broke but the tree went down and there was this '57 Corvette."

"We pulled up in the country and the weeds were growing up 3-4 feet tall and I said, 'Where's the car?'" the elder Yager recalled.

The Yagers plan to leave the tattered interior as it is.

The elusive fiberglass two-seater was a solid representative of one of the most popular years of Corvette models. Its colors were an attractive red-and-white scheme and the white hardtop was definitely an added bonus.

On the drive over to see the car, questions were spinning through the elder Yager's mind, from the condition of the car to its options. Some of those questions were answered with the opening of the barn door, but from its steel shed tomb, some mysteries remained. Blake's mind also spun through the possible secrets kept by the nearly forgotten straight-axle Corvette.

"The first thing that crossed my mind when I saw the car was, I wonder if this car has a race history," Blake said. "Does it have the correct engine? Could it be an 'air box' 1957? All the stuff most Corvette guys will ask themselves when they find an old car that hasn't been touched in many years."

It would be a while before all of the Yagers' questions would be answered. First, they had to determine whether they wanted to buy the car. Once the question was answered with a definitive "yes," it had to be moved, but that wouldn't be an easy task. The car had been placed in the barn in the early to mid 1970s on a homemade trailer made from pipe, and its tires were flat. To move the car, additional devices would have to be employed.

The next morning, with a rollback tow truck at hand, the Yagers aired up the trailer's tires and managed to pull the Corvette from its hiding place of approximately 40 years.

"We had to clear debris to get the trailer out and we just winched it all — car and trailer — on the back of a rollback trailer," Mike Yager said. "As we were extracting the car, I was half expecting a neighbor to say,

'What are you doing?' The guy didn't have a title [handy], so the whole time, I was looking over my shoulder.'"

With the assurance the seller would produce a title, the father-son team had the Corvette driven to their shop so they could figure out exactly what they had bought.

"Driving down the road, there was 35 years of dirt and crap blowing off the car," Mike said. Then there was the question of how to get the Corvette and its trailer off the back of the rollback tow truck. They decided to use a forklift to lift the pairing, drive the rollback out from beneath its load, then lower the Corvette and trailer to the ground together.

With the Corvette safely on the ground, the Yagers began looking for clues to the car's past and researching its original configuration. They learned it was a relatively early Corvette (number 1,258 of 6,339 built) and originally carried an automatic behind its standard four-barrel-equipped 283-cid V-8. A few teeth from the grille had been removed and the interior showed other custom tastes of a previous owner.

"It came from California, and in the '50s and '60s, it was very typical to take your car down to Tijuana and have [diamond-tuft] seat covers installed," Mike said. Fortunately, the original red upholstery appears to remain under the 40-plus-year-old "south of the border" seat covers, although the Yagers have no idea what condition the original seats are in beneath. And they will probably never know.

"When we got the car home, I started thinking about it and put it on social media [websites]," Mike said. "I said we were going to wash the car and people started responding, saying don't wash the car, leave it as it is. We have not attempted to get the car running; we haven't attempted to do anything but put the car on display. We never washed it and we are just going to display it as it is."

In its dusty, dirty state, the car offers endless possibilities and inspires infinite day dreams to those who gaze upon the Illinois earth still covering the stainless, chrome and paint. It also allows the Yagers to share the barn find experience with all who see it.

"We put it out at Corvette Funfest [2010] as its first public display, and you just stood around and listened to all the things people would say about the car," Mike Yager said. "It's a great conversation piece. This one has a better story with it than one that is restored. It just makes the mind wonder. The cool thing about any barn find, you wonder, why did they park it? What was wrong with it? Why did it get put away? Well, a week turned into a month, a month turned into a year.

"It can always be restored," Yager said. "It is kind of like an original — a car can only be original once — and it will only be a barn find once. Once I wash it, it will just be a clapped-out, parts-missing Corvette."

Yager admits that if the car had been an ultra-rare, high-performance Corvette, such as an airbox car or a fuel-injected car, his philosophy might differ.

In some ways, Yager is fortunate the car is a run-of-the-mill Corvette. Not only does he have a great story, he can illustrate it while leaning against the archeological dig. Best of all, it's a story he shares with his son.

"The fun of it is telling the story — it's like any quest for something," Yager said. "I would do this everyday. You really get the adrenaline pumping. I am sure that anybody that has gone on a barn find expedition would tell you the same story. You never know what you are going to find.

"Doing stuff with your children is pretty cool and normally, a lot of people aren't blessed to have their children involved with their business and hobby, but with Blake being involved, it made it so much more special," Yager said.

"I think the barn find was greatly enhanced by being able to experience it with my father," Blake Yager said. "Being able to look at that car and have the memories of walking through the thick weeds and overgrown trees, down to a rusted-out old shed and having to cut a tree down to even get into the shed will always be a pretty neat memory in my eyes every time I think about this car."

By Gregg D. Merksamer

SMALL WONDER

Rare Lancia Appia comes out of hiding

Only about 853 Lancia Appias were built for the 1958 model year, which makes this unique car an unlikely barn find.

If one were seeking proof that sheet metal patina has achieved prestige and not just acceptance at old car shows, they would surely find it in the popular Barn Find exhibits featured at the Fairfield County Concours d'Elegance in Connecticut each September. Though the 2011 display also touted a 1931 Cadillac V-16, a 1938 Bugatti Type 57 and a 1952 Cunningham C-3 coupe, true connoisseurs of the eccentric couldn't help but be entranced by a relatively humble 1958 Lancia Appia Berlina shown by Mike Space of Coopersburg, Pa.

In the absence of sheer size or CCCA

Full Classic stage presence, this trim little sedan - measuring 158 inches overall with a 98.8-inch wheelbase and 46.5-inch tread at each axle — derived its curb appeal from forward-thinking design abetted by careful engineering, epitomized by a pillar-less unibody combining easy entry/egress with the sort of structural stiffness that still allowed all four doors to shut solidly after 53 years and 85,000 miles (being made of aluminum, they inevitably outlast the steel body). Mechanically minded spectators were similarly impressed by the vibration-free idle of the Appia's 1089 CC (66 cubic inch) V-4 motor, which employed compact, 10-degree spacing between each cylinder bank and a lightweight alloy head with hemispherical combustion chambers and inclined overhead valves, operated by twin camshafts mounted in the alloy crank case.

The car is still in its "as found" condition, which made it an interesting sight for show-goers at the Fairfield County Concours d'Elegance in Connecticut.

Calling it "sometimes a job, sometimes a hobby," Space recalled that he started dabbling in British and Italian autos even before he'd "barely graduated" from Scarsdale, New York's high school back in 1968.

When the original "Series 1" Appia debuted at the Turin Motor Show in April 1953, it was positioned - through a switch to solid beam rear axle with outboard brakes - as a smaller, less-costly sibling of the V-6 Lancia Aurelia launched in 1950. Space's Appia, a "Series 2" of the sort unveiled at the March, 1956 Geneva Show, enhanced the model with a 3-centimenter (1.2-inch) wheelbase stretch and a slight bump in horsepower from 38 to 42. The 1959-63 "Series 3" cars had the same trunk and back window as the 2nd, but they were both different from the 1st series. The Only visual difference was from the windshield forward.

While a little more than 98,000 Appia Berlinas - 20,005 Series 1s, 22,424 Series 2s, and 55,577 Series 3s - were sold worldwide before the front-drive, "flat" four Flavia became Lancia's volume four-door, they were never a common sight in the U.S., where the 1946-90 Standard Catalog of American Cars calculates just 853 Lancias of all kinds were sold in 1958. At this time, an Appia Berlina's $2,850 port-of-entry price made it nine dollars more expensive than a V-8 Chevrolet Impala convertible, but a two-for-one bargain versus a top-of-the-line Lancia Flaminia four-door costing $5,998. "Given all their over-engineering," Space declares, "a Lancia is more like a little Mercedes than a big Fiat." One Fairfield spectator who agreed was Jerry McCarthy, once employed as the service manager for a Waterbury, Connecticut Lancia dealer called The Import Motors in the 1950s. "It was a very expensive car for the time," he remembered, "but the only other thing I've ever worked on with the same precision of fit-and-finish was a Rolls. The place I worked for was affiliated with Max Hoffman's import dealership in Manhattan. If you distributed anything of Hoffman's, you distributed everything. If you wanted a Porsche, you had to take two of these and figure out how to sell it."

Calling it "sometimes a job, sometimes a hobby," Space recalled that he started dabbling in British and Italian autos even before he'd "barely graduated" from Scarsdale, New York's high school back in 1968.

"I ran an A35 Austin as my first car," which must have turned a few heads in spite of the inroads made by Beetles, MGs, Volvos and Mercedes-Benz models in this affluent, import-friendly suburb, and it wasn't long before a classmate stepped up and declared "have I got a car for you! It was a 1955 Lancia Aurelia B20 coupe with the paint peeling off it in the back of a neighbor's driveway," but the sheer sophistication of its 60-degree hemi-head V-6, all-independent suspension and inboard rear drum

brakes - not to mention simple, elegant fastback bodywork that seemed impervious to aging if not rusting - made him a fan of the marque for life. "Lancias are a disease that can be contagious," he was warning Fairfield Concours spectators four-plus decades later, "and it's almost impossible to own only one."

This latter assertion was further emphasized by the circumstances under which his Appia was originally obtained around 2005 from fellow Lancia fan Ronendra Mukherjee, who had about a dozen different examples stashed "in a vast leaky shed in a very spooky part of the New Jersey Pine Barrens. This was real 'War of the Worlds' country, and I'd occasionally go down there with a trailer so that I could bring one of his cars home and work on it overnight." When a repair bill on Ronendra's PF 2000 Flavia "far exceeded his ability to pay it," Mike "took three Appia sedans and a bunch of parts he had kicking around in partial trade for the work." Even if its earlier history could only be deduced from the AAA Southern California sticker on the rear bumper, it was obvious this Appia stood out from the other two as being "about as rust free as any Italian car of that vintage could be," since "it had thankfully been stored in a nice dry corner" of that spooky Pine Barrens shed. "If I restored it," Mike nonetheless recalled debating as he pondered its otherwise "delightfully ratty" condition, "no one would know just how solid it had been," on top of which the finished car would still be "almost worthless" and "would look like all the other Lancia Appia Berlinas you see every day." Joking aside, the other two "hopelessly trashed" cars yielded "a wealth of mechanical and unobtainable parts that allowed me to revive this puppy to a very sweet driving condition, including one transmission out of six that actually had a good first gear."

Though he ultimately chose to trailer his Appia to Fairfield - "I was originally going to drive this up, but I'm still working a few bugs out after 400 miles on the road" — Mike confirmed "it'll cruise along just fine, barring a driveshaft vibration above 65 miles an hour," which really could be taken as a hint that its 80 mph-or-so top speed is approaching anyway. Back home in Coopersburg, he added, "all I have to do is turn left out of my driveway, and I'm on some gorgeous driving roads," where a column-shifted four-speed gearbox "you have to shift with your fingertips" ensures "it's not bad as a hill climber," especially as the engine has been "a little souped up" by cherry-picking "all the best parts from the Appias I had." Even if the Aurelia B24 Spyder, Flaminia coupe, and Zagato-bodied GTs will always be the Lancias that command the most money in collector circles, Mike believes the firm's Berlinas "are their best-kept secret, the most-solid and nicest driving of all the Lancias. In Italy, you might say these are their most simpatico offerings, demonstrating true sympathy and empathy between the car and the driver."

Story and photos by Sharon Thatcher

SAD MEMORIES GONE GOOD

Happy days are here again for once-forlorn '61 'Vette

Gary Janssen's 1961 Corvette was battered and blue when he pulled it from a friend's barn in 2002.

There is truth to the old adage that good things come to those who wait. Take the case of the 1961 Corvette that sat wasting away in a farm shed in north central Wisconsin. It took 16 years for the old car to see the light of day again, but thanks to the patience of one man, the rewards have been plentiful. It's been a happy ending for both the car and the man who restored it.

Gary Janssen, of Merrill, Wis., said the car belonged to a friend of his when he first saw it, but it wasn't for sale. "It belonged to his brother who had passed away," he said of the previous owner. It took awhile for the

The old Corvette had seen better days, and it lost an eye in a mishap when it was pulled from its barn.

family to let go. "It was a memory and they didn't want to get rid of it, but they didn't like to see it deteriorating."

The time wasn't right for Janssen, either. Although he never stopped thinking about the Corvette and the possibilities, his own life was too consumed with making a living and raising a family to adopt an old car that had 98,000 miles on its odometer and needed a serious restoration. Still, he often inquired about the Corvette and offered to help fix it up if ever the family decided to take on the expense.

Then, one day in 2002, everything fell in place. "After the kids were out of college, then it was my time," Janssen said. Instead of selling the Corvette to someone who was interested in parting it out, the owner decided to sell it to Janssen for restoration.

By then, the car was 16 years older and in sadder shape than the first time Janssen had laid eyes on it. "It had chicken manure in the carpeting, fruit jars all over it and tractor tires leaning on it," he said. Still, to Janssen it was a beautiful sight.

His farmer friend hooked onto the car with his tractor to pull it out of the shed, when Janssen's joy was suddenly dimmed by calamity. As the car was being pulled from the barn with a chain, it began to roll forward down a slight embankment and collided with the back end of the tactor, damaging the car's passenger-side headlight assembly, grille and body.

Disappointed, but not deterred, Janssen trailered the car home and immediately began the restoration process. "I started it in 2002," he said. "We finished in 2004-2005," explaining that the "we" included his son Cliff. "Cliff helped a little bit when he could be here. He was in college and he'd come back and we'd tackle it together." Gary's wife Cindy was a strong supporter, "and she paid the bills."

Janssen set one goal for himself when he started the project: "I said, once I start it, I want to continue. I didn't want to stop, because you see so many projects that get started and then get put in a corner. They're in the corner and then you fall out of love with it."

To avoid the corner, he set up one ground rule. "I said to myself, 'When I go into the garage, I have to do one thing; it doesn't matter how much or how big a thing, even if it's just polishing one stainless part, do one thing.'"

He lived up to his vow, and he never found the corner and he never fell out of love with his project.

Even though the Corvette was the first car Janssen had ever restored, he was by no means a total rookie. "I'm an electrician, but years ago I was a mechanic — a welder," he said. He had also been a farmer and knew a thing or two about machinery. The Internet, magazines and friends in the car hobby were also invaluable resources. "We touched every nut and bolt about four times," he figures.

The 'Vette received a total restoration and a new coat of white paint. It wasn't the first time the car had been repainted!

The 1961 Corvette as it looks today.

Perhaps the biggest surprise during the restoration was the discovery of the car's original color. "The color was white originally," Janssen said. "I thought it was green because when we started to sand the blue away there was green underneath. It had been painted twice before."

The Corvette was returned to its original white with the blue side cove. "We researched it and it was an option, so we just flew with it," he said. The paint job was done by a professional in nearby Wausau.

The car was authentically restored with a few exceptions. Because of a knee replacement a few years back, Janssen installed a different shifter. In the interior is a new dash pad to replace the old sun-cracked dash.

"I also put disc brakes on because the original single-cylinder [master cylinder], even though I rebuilt it, the rubber was going bad," he explained. "This allows me a dual-cylinder braking system. You've got all this money invested, if you trailer it from show to show, it's different; and I respect those guys who do, but they have to respect me as well."

Under the hood, there's a new radiator. "A friend of mine is a radiator guy and he said the old radiator is fine, but it's 40-some years old. If you want to drive it, do you want to be broke down by the side the road?"

But more importantly, and more prone to debate, is the 350-cid crate engine installed to accommodate today's lower fuel octane ratings. He knows it disappoints some purists. "A lot of Corvette guys don't agree with what I did," he said, "But I have the original radiator and the original motor in the garage, so if we did want to change it,

it only takes a couple of hours to change it, but we just enjoy going out with it and we want to be safe."

The car does indeed go out a lot. The Janssens take it to several car shows throughout the summer and have added about 11,000 miles to the odometer since finishing the restoration. "It does have its dings now," he admits, "but we enjoy owning it and the fun part is driving it."

New, Janssen's car was at the low-end price for a Corvette. "This was a Plain Jane," he said. "A solid white car with a [230-hp] 283, four-barrel — the smallest V-8 you could put into a Corvette. It did have a radio and a heater. I think they ran about $3,200-$3,400." Roughly 9,600 were built for 1961.

Back when the car sat neglected in a farm shed, it may have been a Plain Jane, but today, Janssen's Corvette is anything but a wallflower. It gets plenty of looks and plenty of trophies. "I don't go for trophies," Janssen said about car shows. "I enjoy talking to people and it just happens; the trophies just seem to follow me home."

By Brian Earnest

SEEING THE LIGHT

After 27 years couped up in a cramped Florida garage, this amazing 1965 Cadillac has never looked better

In 2011, Bob Mayer became the second owner of this 1965 Cadillac Sedan DeVille. The car hadn't moved since 1983, but today the low-mileage survivor is back on the road.

Bob Mayer makes no bones about it: he loves original automobiles. Low-mileage, unrestored, intact cars are right in his wheelhouse.

The well-known, retired Miami television newsman has had his share of such cars in the past, but he's never had one that was as stunningly original as the sweet 1965 Cadillac Sedan DeVille that he uncovered — literally — last spring. He's also never had a car that was as dirty and … uh … aromatic as the hulking Caddy. Fortunately, Mayer doesn't mind putting up with a little cleaning and elbow grease when it comes to

"But for the original owner, this was not just a car to him. He definitely babied it. He only drove it on the weekend. He had another car that he drove for work and during the week."

his cars, especially when the diamond that needs to be polished is as flawless as his '65 DeVille.

"Well, it was filthy, but I've always been able to see through dirt and see through detailing," said Mayer. "I knew I could make this car look good."

Of course, it isn't overly surprising that a car with only 24,000 original miles on the odometer could be in fantastic shape. The question is how such a beautiful car sat untouched in a cramped garage for 27 years without moving an inch. The slumber was so lengthy and so strange that it almost scared Mayer away from even coming to look at the car.

Almost.

"Well, I saw the ad for the car, but I didn't go look at it at first. I let it sit there for, I dunno, a month or 6 weeks because I was just never involved in getting a car that didn't run," Mayer said. "And it was made clear that this car didn't run in 27 years. But I kept seeing the ad, and I said, 'You know what, I'm going to see if I can call this guy and see where he is and if maybe I can get somebody to look at the car. ...[Finally]

I decided to go look at the car, and I took a battery charger and jumper cables and compressor to blow up the tires — I took a whole bunch of stuff with me.

"When he took the car, opened up the garage door and it was dank and smelly and you could tell that no one had been there in a long time. The house there was empty. The man's mom had lived there but she had been put in nursing home … When he opened the garage, there was a strong mildew smell. But then he turned on the light and it looked like a brand new car! … It was in this cramped garage. It had barely had 2 or 3 inches clearance around the car. I asked if I could get the car outside, so the two of us pushed the car back, got it outside and my jaw dropped. It was just spectacular."

Within a few minutes, Mayer had the jumper cables hooked up from his car to the tired old Cadillac so he could check some of the accessories and the car's electrical system. "I didn't try to start the car, which was probably a good thing, but I hooked up the battery to the battery on my '06 Cadillac and we started testing things, and to our astonishment, everything worked! We were

This Caddy's big 429-cid V-8 wasn't stuck, but it needed help after it's long slumber.

both totally astonished. I turned on the radio and it turned right on. I couldn't get a station, but then I remembered the station tuner — if you pushed it in the antenna goes up. So I pushed it in and wall-lah, the antenna goes up, and it starts playing! The six-way power seats worked, the turn signals, everything worked on the car. And at this point I'm started to get excited."

The original owner of the car was no doubt excited about the car when he first laid eyes on it, too. The big sedan was ordered in October of 1964 and picked up as a "VIP delivery" at the Cadillac headquar-

ters in Brooklyn, N.Y., on March 15, 1965. The car's window price was $6,898.65, but the first owner paid only $6,086 — perhaps getting a discount because of the long delay. After such a long wait for his car, the man apparently showed great restraint in his use of the Caddy, accumulating just 24,000 miles over the next 17 years before he died in 1983.

"These VIP purchases, if you knew somebody, you could do back then. You could pick the car up at the factory," Mayer said. "In the owner's manual, where it lists selling dealer, it says Cadillac Motor Divi-

The exterior of the Caddy remains in near-perfect condition.

sion. But for the original owner, this was not just a car to him. He definitely babied it. He only drove it on the weekend. He had another car that he drove for work and during the week."

And when the man died, his widow was clearly in no hurry to let anybody else have

his car. "She had the battery removed and didn't let anybody near the car," Mayer said.

The lovely blue and white Cadillac was one of 45,535 hardtop four-door DeVilles built for the 1965 model year. The DeVilles were also available as four-door sedans, two-door hardtop coupes and two-door convertibles, with the two hardtop models being by far the most popular with new car buyers of the day.

The Cadillacs received some dramatic styling changes for 1965. Gone were the last vestiges of the tail fins that once defined the cars. The body lines were more sharply defined, the bodies were slightly wider, and the engines were moved forward six inches on new perimeter frames.

And up front was perhaps the most obvious change — the stacked headlights. The vertical arrangement was all new and would last for four model years before the side-by-side look returned for 1969.

The DeVilles continued with a wheelbase length of 129.5 inches, and the holdover 429-cid, 340-hp four-barrel V-8 was back under the hood.

The 1965 model year marked the 16th year for the nameplate in the Cadillac menu. In 1965, Series 62 was discontinued and the DeVille became part of the Calais series, resting between the base Calais and top-end Fleetwood lineup.

Mayer had never owned a 1965 DeVille before, but he had definitely found one he wanted. The question then was how much

was the car worth? It definitely wasn't drivable, and the effects of such a lengthy slumber were unknown.

"I pulled the gas cap and whoa! That was probably the strongest varnish smell I ever smelled," Mayer said. "Of course, this did present a new set of problems, because I knew that some other things would have to be done.

"I tried to buy the car real cheap, but he wouldn't hear of it. So I waited a couple of weeks, and in the meantime I talked to my mechanic ... He said he wasn't concerned about getting the motor running. Those big 429 motors should be fine, but he rattled off a lot of things I would have to do to it, starting with the gas tank. He read off just a litany of parts and labor scenarios. But I decided to try again to buy the car. It had been on eBay, but he didn't get a single bid on it. People were scared off because it hadn't run in so long.

"I finally told the guy, 'This is a magnificent car, but it has been so neglected. I can't give you what your asking for it' ... but we eventually worked out a deal."

Fortunately, the engine was not frozen, and Mayer's mechanic had the car running in short order. "We had to use a gas can

The original owner of the car was no doubt excited about the car when he first laid eyes on it, too.

Mayer had a battle on his hands to rid the car of a moldy smell.

for the gas, because of the problems with the gas tank, but it really ran pretty nicely before he did anything else. Even the carburetor — it was on the list of things to do — but he basically just had to clean it. We didn't even replace it."

Mayer eventually replaced the radiator core, gas tank and fuel lines, sending unit, brake and wheel cylinders, master cylinder, all of the belts and hoses and the tires. "I was able to save the A/C hoses — they are still original," he said. "And the compressor is actually the original compressor. It still had a charge after 27 years! Not much, but

it had a charge. Now, it's blowing ice cold air."

One of the biggest challenges, he said, has been ridding the car of the moldy smell that had settled in after so many years in a tiny garage. The Cadillac looks like a new car, but doesn't exactly smell like one. "At this point, I'm open to suggestions," he said with a laugh. "I've literally washed the carpet three times to try to get the smell out, and get rid of that 'mist' that sort of settles on the interior."

Mayer has replaced some rubber around the windows, but he doesn't foresee any other repairs in the Caddy's immediate future. He's had the car on the road for several months now, and so far it has passed every test. "My wife and I drove it down to Homestead for breakfast the other day. Driving it was just like going back in time!" he said. "I've been collecting cars for 30-plus years. I've got seven cars and I've never had a car this original and this nice. It's just amazing. It runs just like a new car."

"And this car is probably the most documented car I've ever had. Even though [the owner] died 27 years ago and even though she was a little over the top about letting anybody near the car, she saved all the documentation. I've got the window sticker, all of the owner's manuals and paperwork, the protector plate with the father's name on it ... Everything that you could possibly get when you get a new Cadillac was in a folder, and I love that kind of stuff! This thing is a passion of mine. If I'm not working, I'm busy with my cars. I don't do any major mechanical work, but I love being with my cars.

Mayer is planning on another special trip soon — back to see the family that had watched the car sit for so long. "I called him and said I was going to come up and take his family out. I'm sure they'll be very excited to see the car," he said. "This car was always in his life, so it was an emotional thing to let this car go. I'm gonna take the guy and his family out to breakfast so they can see it again back on the road."

Mayer figures the car will make its big show debut not far from his home in Homestead, Fla., for the AACA Winter Meet March 4-5. He doesn't usually get too hung up on show awards, but admits he hopes the judges appreciate the Cadillac half as much as he does. "I'm looking forward to entering this car in the Survivor Class," he said. "I've never entered a car in the AACA Nationals in Survivor, and I think this car is a shoe-in to get an award in this category. The only things that aren't original are the tires!

"I've told the story of this car a million times, but it's kind of exciting to tell people that I brought it back. I get to feel responsible for resuscitating this car and giving it life again."

SOLID GOLD

The Golden Commandos '65 Plymouth altered-wheelbase car survives

Mike Guffey's research showed the Plymouth wore steel wheels almost all season in 1965. BF Goodrich 7.1 x 15 Lifesavers, new old stock, are up front; 10.0 M&H Racemaster slicks — also vintage — are on the rear. Details abound, including the big pin wingnuts, vintage decal remnants, rear window hold-down straps and tune-up specs painted on the firewall.

Vintage race cars often lead hard lives. After whatever fame they attained for their owner, these generally well-used machines began a slow downward spiral. In drag racing, that often means alterations or upgrades desired by subsequent owners, changes that left much of the surviving history on the scrap pile. After they were no longer competitive, they would be parted out for their components and parked someplace where the elements and time slowly returned them to dirt. Once located by someone who understands what the hulk is, the desire to simply "rebody" the entire vehicle is often a serious temptation.

Few drag cars are as widely desired as the original altered-wheelbase hardtops Chrysler created in 1965. That was a sea-

The engine is a vintage 1966 Hemi mill with aluminum heads and all the correct pieces for the Hilborn fuel injection, including a two-gallon Eelco tank, oversize fuel filter and factory-approved belt-driven pump.

Few drag cars are as widely desired as the original altered-wheelbase hardtops Chrysler created in 1965.

son when the MoPar troops were protesting NASCAR rules on the Hemi, and money was redirected toward the quarter-mile. By radically changing the wheelbase beneath the vehicles to move the weight forward, the 11 creations by a Detroit subcontractor named Amblewagon under factory direction became the basis for the term "funny car."

Those cars went to select drivers nationwide. The Plymouth featured here was presented to the Golden Commandos team, which consisted of Plymouth factory engineers, with former corporate lawyer Al "The Lawman" Eckstrand as the driver that year. The team traveled from Detroit only for the largest events, including the notorious first-ever 1965 *Super Stock Magazine* Nationals in York, Pa., that August. NHRA considered this event a literal "drag strip riot," with more than 25,000 fans along the apron of the air-landing-strip-turned-racetrack long past midnight to see some of the sport's biggest names duke it out. When the final for Unlimited Fuel was called, it was none other than Eckstrand against the noted Dodge of "Dandy" Dick Landy. Eckstrand beat the feared Landy's Dodge, a hole shot-assisted 9.67 seconds to a losing 9.58.

The following year, at the same event (held at New York National Speedway in Long Island), it was Commandos team member John Dallifor driving this car. He won the heads-up 2,700-lb. Fuel title on Saturday and then went three rounds in the handicap-style Super Eliminator run-offs on Sunday, clocking a very fast 9.06 on nitro during the losing run. The well-used altered 1965 Plymouth went to a new owner late in 1966 when the team produced a new Barracuda for funny car racing.

The car showed up around Detroit strips painted red and blue as "Mission: Impossible" and then disappeared for over a decade. Collector Steve Atwell eventually met a local Detroit-area Super Stock racer who mentioned his brother owned "a funny-wheelbase car." Atwell saw it and verified it was indeed real "gold," and then spent two years working out a way to buy it. He in turn sold it to the late Dick Towers, a noted historian from Santa Ana, Calif.

I first saw this car in Southern California as a hulk almost 20 years ago at Towers' shop. Dick was a former Classic Lincoln expert with a passion for MoPar drag racing. Like the others in that batch, the Plymouth had been acid-dipped, weakening the

Dick Towers sits behind the wheel of the car that he cared for during a 20-plus-year ownership. Here, he is joined by the crew that helped bring his old car back to the track. Dick's son Richard Towers is next to the door. Dick Towers passed away just weeks after this photo was taken.

body and unitized frame. The floors looked like wrinkled brown paper bags even when new, the roof had nearly fallen off from race fatigue, and I-beams were welded on top of the team's ca.-1965 subframe connectors. Between his growing photo archive and prewar restoration work, Towers worked on it when time allowed, but he was careful not to take any more history from the car than necessary. However, it was Mike Guffey, one of Dick's closest friends, who finally finished the car.

"When Mike came around and began talking about wanting it, and was willing to pay me what I felt this car was worth, I knew it was time to let it go," said Towers

shortly before his death in late 2009. "Some other guys had bugged me about it, but I knew they would have wanted to rebody it; Mike was one of the only people I would have sold this car to."

Guffey is an Indiana race car collector whose willingness to go to extremes to maintain originality is legendary. Guffey had sold the 1965 Landy Dodge, and used some of that money to buy the Commandos car and do it right.

Today, all the vintage fiberglass is original, as is the windshield and rear window. It took 10 hours to carefully cut the I-beams out and grind the welds off the paper-thin floor. After the car was wrecked in 1966, the

An aging NHRA sticker testifies to this car's racing history.

passenger side door had been patched shut with no window frame; Guffy and his guys did re-create that, putting new side glass in the car as well. Foam was sprayed into the roof area, but it's still original.

The original single low-back driver's seat was still intact, though someone had begun adding button-tuft upholstery to it. Kramer Automotive Specialties supplied correct carpet; Gary Ball Reproductions supplied the seat skin, headliner and door panels; and Guffy and friend Troy Fairchild did most of the installation work themselves in Guffy's shop. Indianapolis' Tommy Mitchell is responsible for the paint, while Jim Studinski, a sign guy and pinstriper who once did work for Logghe in Detroit during the 1960s, expertly applied the gold leaf and lettering.

Race car expert Erik Lindberg of Liberty Performance in Minnesota received the car after a static debut in 2008 at the All-Hemi Reunion in Ohio; he built and installed a solid short-block with a correct Hilborn outfit and rare 1965 K-series aluminum heads from Guffey's stash, a reverse valve body TorqueFlite and a 4.56 rear pumpkin. It looked great, and Towers, who had been diagnosed with an untreatable form of cancer, finally got a chance to actually ride in the rare car.

During the Flatlander Fling in Nebraska in 2009, Lindberg strapped in as the pilot, and Towers rode as a passenger in the shotgun seat while the car was driven hard for a few 60-foot launches at Kearney Raceway Park. The car, fragile and original, will never have to prove its worth by running through the lights at speed. To even see it under power was a truly memorable experience. Thanks to the collectors involved, the Golden Commandos 1965 Plymouth is as original as any altered-wheelbase restoration can be, a surviving reflection of the golden age of drag racing.

By Angelo Van Bogart

OUT OF THE BOTTLE

'I Dream of Jeannie' Barris custom appears again

A period shot of the 1969 Pontiac Firebird 400 used in the TV show "I Dream of Jeannie" after George Barris modified the car for its return appearance in the final season of 1970.

Few vintage cars have rubbed tires with as many Hollywood hot shots and hobby heroes early in life as the 1969 Pontiac Firebird 400 convertible co-owned by Chad Brousseau of Salem, Iowa, and Curtis Judd of Brandon, Fla. Like most hulks of iron in that small fraternity, the partners' Firebird was thought to have fallen into history like the TV show in which it was featured.

"Everybody has heard of the Munster Mobile cars and the MonkeeMobile, and this car is one of those that just faded away," Brousseau said. "A lot of people never even heard of it."

Of the unknown number of Firebird 400 convertibles built for the 1969 model year, just one was used as Major Roger Healey's ride in the 1960s TV show "I Dream of Jeannie." Major Healey was played by Bill Daily, who co-starred on the program about an astronaut (Larry Hagman as Major Nelson) who secretly found a genie (Barbara

Eden) and kept her bottled up in his home. Besides its spacey plot, the show was known by gearheads for the cool Ponchos zipping into the screen, all subtly and intentionally placed by Pontiac.

"Major Nelson drove a lot of GTOs, but by 1969, he went to a Bonneville convertible, but Major Healey was driving this Firebird," Brousseau said.

Brousseau's Firebird joined the NBC cast in early 1969 through Jim Wangers, the legendary ad man and marketing genius behind performance at General Motors, especially while with Pontiac in the 1960s. Wangers then helped put the Firebird 400 into the hands of George Barris, the King of Kustomizers before it finally went into

the personal garages of two different Hollywood types.

"It's basically only ever had two owners," said Brousseau. Those owners weren't registered until after the Firebird was done making its small-screen appearances at the end of "I Dream of Jeannie," which ran from 1965 to 1970.

"[Major Healey] drove it around as the 'orange car' for numerous episodes," Brousseau said. "Then Pontiac actually commissioned George Barris to do a one-off on this car, so you would think it looks like a '69 Trans Am convertible — it has side scoops on the quarters, it has the three-piece spoiler on the back — but Barris painted it and it went from the original [Carousel Red] to

"Major Nelson drove a lot of GTOs, but by 1969, he went to a Bonneville convertible, but Major Healey was driving this Firebird."

a color close to Chevy Rally Green, a really deep metallic green color, with white stripes. Then it went back on the show for a couple little brief spots as the 'green car.'"

Through this conversion, and even earlier, Wangers worked behind the scenes to prepare the Firebird 400 for the small screen.

"In those days, the cars turned over to the shows came out of the advertising and sales promotion budgets," Wangers said. "And so that would be a decision that would be approved by the ad manager, and in this case, the general manager, John Delorean."

Since Wangers worked closely with Delorean on marketing matters with Pontiac, he also remembers placing Pontiacs on the '60s TV shows "My Three Sons" and "Surfside 6." Of all those Pontiacs, the "I Dream of Jeannie" Firebird 400 stands apart because of its flashy Carousel Red color.

"I am responsible for getting [the 'I Dream of Jeannie' car] Carousel Red," Wangers said. "We were building that Carousel Red color from the start of production in 1969, because that was the Chevrolet color Hugger Orange. We were building all the Firebirds and Camaros out of the Norwood plant near Cincinnati. Because they were on the same production line, for a very minimal cost, we could build a car using a Chevrolet color."

As Wangers explained it, anyone could order a Carousel Red Firebird or Firebird 400, but few people did. As a result, the "I Dream of Jeannie" Firebird 400 convertible was somewhat unique.

"It was as clear as the nose on your face on the order form, except nobody read them; the salesman didn't even read them," Wangers said. "We did a hell of a lot to help [the color] when we put the car on that show. We were very proud, because there weren't many Firebirds around in that color."

The use of Carousel Red on the "I Dream of Jeannie" Firebird did a small but notable part to preview a special Pontiac GTO that would be released in April 1969 bearing "The Judge" name. The Judge would be heavily promoted in Carousel Red, but offered in any color Pontiac offered. In anticipation of the upcoming "The Judge" edition of the 1969 GTO, Wangers said the use of Carousel Red on Firebirds was suspended in early 1969 so the color would be exclusive in the Pontiac line to The Judge.

"As a factory, we did not want to put a Trans Am on 'Jeannie,' because we had that Carousel Red Firebird there and that was helping us with promoting The Judge, which was so identified with that Carousel Red."

Keeping Major Healey behind the wheel of a new Firebird became complicated in

The interior and drive train of the Pontiac were left stock, including the 330-hp, 400-cid V-8.

late 1969. As Wangers tells it, the delays in getting the 1970 Camaros and Firebirds were partially responsible for having the "I Dream of Jeannie" 1969 Firebird 400 freshened for the 1970 show season.

"We turned it over to George Barris, who had been knocking on our door to do business with us," Wangers said. "We actually 'stole' the car at the request of the production company. When the car got turned over to Barris, he started to customize it."

Carousel Red was no longer offered on The Judge in 1970, so changing the color no longer affected Pontiac's promotional efforts. That allowed Barris to borrow styling features from the 1969 Pontiac Trans Am, a car Pontiac chose not to feature earlier on the TV show.

"[Barris] did a nice little deviation on the stripes off a '69 Trans Am and then that car got involved in quite a few configurations, but I was no longer involved," Wangers said.

Not all of Barris' inspiration for the modifications undertaken on the "I Dream of Jeannie" Firebird 400 date to the 1969 Trans Am. As Wangers also recalls, a few of the car's features date to 1968, when Barris built a run of special Firebirds for another TV program.

"There was a TV show done in '68 ('Sounds of '68') and they did a Superteen Firebird giveaway and [Barris] built three Superteen Firebirds for it with a similar kind of hood and a similar spoiler, but a more radical front end [than the 'I Dream of Jeannie' Firebird]."

Compared to the Superteen 1968 Firebird 400s built by Barris, the "I Dream of Jeannie" 1969 Firebird 400 is closer to stock, lacking the electronics in the backseat of the Superteen cars, which featured a typewriter, television set and tape deck. Brousseau finds the lack of such components in the "I Dream of Jeannie" car as a plus.

"The nice thing about this car is the interior is left stock and [its modifications are limited to] the outside body mods," Brousseau said. According to one source, Brousseau said the relatively minor modifications performed by Barris on the "I Dream of Jeannie" car totaled $130,000, a hefty sum for the time and enough to buy a fleet of more than 25 similarly equipped Firebird 400 convertibles.

At the conclusion of Barris' work and then the show, Brousseau learned the mildly customized Firebird 400 was bought by the show's art director for his daughter at a loss to Pontiac.

"She drove it for a while, and I guess they lived in an area of Beverly Hills," Brousseau said. From there, it caught the eye of the son of movie producer Mace Neufeld, associated with such films as "Clear and Present Danger" and "The Omen."

"[Neufeld's] son had known the car and had ridden by the house it was stored in on his bicycle, and he stopped in and asked them about the car, and he got his dad to buy it in 1977," Brousseau said. "It was his car in high school and college."

Any Pontiac Firebird 400 convertible makes an enviable ride on campus, especially a car with touches by a famous customizer. But by 1986, the shine had worn off the four-wheeled former TV star. At that time, Neufeld's son, now a respected Hollywood type in his own right, bottled up his special Firebird 400 convertible wherever he could find storage. In 2009, he placed the car for sale on an Internet site.

Brousseau and his partner spotted the car for sale, but there were no photographs with the ad. Like many of the Pontiac fans eyeing the car, Brousseau and his partner speculated on whether the car was authentic. Eventually, the ad disappeared until spring 2011 when it re-appeared, this time with pictures. Within an hour of spotting it, Brousseau and his partner jumped on the car and began the process of authenticating it with Pontiac Historic Services.

"When I sent off for the PHS documentation, I got a phone call the next day," Brousseau said. "In all my years of sending in PHS VIN numbers, I have never gotten a call from Jim Mattison the next day."

Brousseau learned the Pontiac is unusual because it has three build sheets: the first shows the car's assembly date and its long list of options: special-order Carousel Red paint, wood steering wheel with power tilt function, power antenna, power steering, power top, power disc brakes, console, Rally II wheels, remote mirror, power windows, deluxe seat belts, air conditioning, Rally gauges and more. The build sheet showed a total price of $4,877 reflecting nearly $1,800 in options to the Firebird convertible's $3,083 price.

"The first invoice is dated January 1969, and had it billed to the zone office in Michigan," Brousseau said. "Then it had a second build sheet directing it to the zone office in Los Angeles, and from there, it went to the production company of 'I Dream of Jeannie.'

"When the show ended, the third build sheet is actually dated the very end of July of 1970, so like a year and a half after it was produced, it was still owned by Pontiac. The MSO was issued in 1970, and there is a charged loss to this account and the final invoice is a dollar."

In addition to numerous build sheets, the Firebird 400 has endured additional coats of paint over its body. By Brousseau's count, it sports three re-paints over its original Carousel Red, starting with Barris' green-with-white-stripes scheme to the blue-with-white-stripes job for the art director's daughter to the white-with-blue-stripes scheme for the producer's son. Amazingly, the Barris additions remain under the paint layers, from the unique non-functional dual-snorkel hood to the quarter-panel scoops to the three-piece rear spoiler. Unfortunately, the Barris paint scheme, which included painting the tail panel white, is buried under the more recent repaints.

The fact that the Firebird spent its life in California certainly helped keep it the solid and intact specimen that it remains, although Brousseau notes it deserves a restoration. When he found it, the car had been stored outdoors after the seller lost storage in his father's garage and a friend's building. If Brousseau didn't already have a 1970 Pontiac GTO Ram Air 455 hardtop under restoration, he would probably keep the unique Firebird for his own collection. But it's just not in the cards.

"I would love to have it, but a car like that, a one-off car, it needs to be taken to someone and be totally restored into a trailer queen," Brousseau said. "It's worth a lot of money, and I would really rather drive my '70 Impala and hit a water puddle and not have to cringe."

In the meantime, Brousseau is having fun authenticating the car and piecing together its history.

"It is kind of like a trifecta," Brousseau said. "It was a special car built by Pontiac, then it was a TV car, then it was a one-off George Barris custom car."

Rarely does it get better than that.

The raised twin hood scoops were part of the Barris body mod's.

Story and photos by Larry Bell

JUDGE MYTH
IS DISROBED

Reader finds locally famous GTO right under his nose

After this 1969 GTO The Judge disappeared from the streets of New Castle, Ind., in 1972, rumors persisted about its fate.

In March 1969, I was 17 years old and driving a new Verdoro Green 1968 Pontiac GTO convertible with a four-speed. I felt I was the "coolest cat" on the street. One late night, while "cruising Broad" in search of girls or a late-night street race, I noticed another GTO pull up behind me as I sat at a red light.

This GTO was orange, but I wasn't aware Pontiac made an orange GTO. Then, as the light was ready to turn green, the driver lunged the car up beside me at the light, blipped the throttle and proceeded to give me the "let's go" sign — he wanted to race. I was so stunned by the car — it said "The Judge" on the fender — that I froze. He took off, smoking the tires of the bright-orange GTO The Judge, and I was left sitting at the light. Feeling like yesterday's news, I turned right and went home, all the while wondering what The Judge was. The next day, I found out what a GTO The Judge was, but I never laid eyes on that particular car for another 40 years.

In 1983, I was working out at a local gym when a young girl noticed my GTO T-shirt and she told me about her uncle's Judge. Apparently, he had parked it in 1972 with a bad clutch and never drove it again. The girl also told me her uncle's name and where they lived, but after quite a few attempts, I was never able to contact the owners.

Many more years passed and by this time, this particular The Judge was becoming a local urban legend, a ghost of sorts. Stories about the car circulated for decades, most saying it had been sold, destroyed or was stored at the edge of town in a shack and guarded by a pack of wolves. No one seemed to know where the elusive Pontiac had vanished to all those years ago, and the owners apparently weren't talking either.

In April 2009, I was sitting in a little diner I own and having breakfast with a friend of mine when three older women sat

OCW reader Larry Bell eventually found it hidden in a local garage in 2009.

In 1983, I was working out at a local gym when a young girl noticed my GTO T-shirt and she told me about her uncle's Judge.

down at the next booth. The Highway 38 Diner is car-themed and the walls are covered with pictures of my cars, both current and past. One of the ladies asked if the cars on the wall were mine and I said, "Yes, most of them." The lady then asked me, "How much is a one-lady-owned '69 GTO The Judge with a four-speed worth?"

I nearly dropped my fork and said, "You have got to be Donna." She said yes, she was, and she was interested in the value, because someone had recently approached her to buy the car for $8,000. Donna said she thought the price was low, and it was. I told her what I would pay for the car sight-unseen, and she thanked me for being honest in telling her what I thought it was worth.

I also told Donna how I had seen the car once — 40 years ago — and had searched for it unsuccessfully for 25 years. I said I would love to add it to my collection. She made it plain the car belonged to her, not her husband, and how she paid for the car herself and drove it off the showroom floor at Wells Pontiac in Richmond, Ind., in 1969. It was solely her decision what to do with the car.

Two days later, she left a message at the diner for me to call her. I immediately called and made an appointment to look at the long-lost The Judge as soon as I got over the flu. She told me not to worry, the car was mine if I wanted it, but we still hadn't agreed on a price. After a few agonizing days, I was healthy enough to get my first look at this "urban legend" in more than 40 years. And it turns out this storied car was just six blocks from my New Castle, Ind., home!

When I laid eyes on The Judge for the second time, it was parked in the same tiny garage where it had been left since 1972 and had not seen daylight since. The car had a little more than 40,000 miles on the odometer, new tires, new exhaust and a 1972 Indiana State Safety Inspection sticker. Donna and I agreed on a price in a matter of minutes and the long-lost The Judge was finally mine.

I took a crew to examine The Judge, and we were all amazed at how well the car had survived the decades. We filled the four flat tires with air, lifting it off of can of house paint, then wiggled the Hurst shifter a few times and pulled it out of the garage and onto a trailer for a short trip to a friends' restoration shop to see what we had. After a few days of cleaning, it came back to life cosmetically and began to look as it did in '72.

The gas tank was emptied (it was as clean as new); the carburetor was rebuilt; the plugs, plug wires and points were changed; fresh oil was poured in the crankcase; the battery was changed; and with a few other minor items, The Judge started right up. It also turns out the clutch was fine after all.

After 37 years of hiding, The Judge was alive again, purring like a tiger. I have taken it to a couple local shows in the last 18 months and everyone remembers the car and has a story to tell about it. It is a true survivor and will never be restored or sold.

Today, the 40,000-mile The Judge looks as fine as when it was parked in 1972.

Flashy Judge could hand out swift justice

Any muscle car inspired by the "Here Come da Judge" skits on Rowan & Martin's "Laugh-In" TV show was sure to be a bit crazy, and the GTO The Judge was crazy in a very fast way. As *Car Life* magazine once put it, "Pontiac inspired the supercar for this generation . . . and The Judge is one of the best."

The new model of GTO was designed to be what *Car and Driver* magazine called an "econo racer." However, the end product became a heavily optioned muscle car priced at more than $300 over the GTO's sticker and still provided a lot of muscle for the money. It was a machine that could race "as delivered," and for a lot less money than a purpose-built drag racing car.

Pontiac Motor Division's release of the "The Judge" option package was made on Dec. 19, 1968. At first, "The Judge" came only in Carousel Red with tri-color striping, but it was later made available in the full range of colors that were available for other '69 GTOs. Special standard features of The Judge package included a blacked-out grille, Rally II wheels (minus bright trim

rings), functional hood scoops and "The Judge" decals on the sides of the front fenders and "Ram Air" decals on the hood scoops. At the rear of the car there was a 60-inch-wide "floating" deck lid airfoil with a "The Judge" decal emblem on the upper right-hand surface.

The standard "The Judge" engine was the Pontiac-built 400-cid/366-hp Ram Air III V-8. It came linked to a three-speed manual transmission with a floor-mounted Hurst T-handle shifter and a 3.55:1 rear axle. A total of 8,491 GTOs and Judges were sold with this motor and only 362 of them were convertibles. The more powerful 400-cid/370-hp Ram Air IV engine was installed in 759 cars in the same two lines and 59 of these cars were convertibles.

"The Judge" option was added to 6,725 GTO two-door hardtops and only 108 GTO ragtops. The editors of *Car Life* magazine whipped The Judge through the quarter-mile at 14.45 seconds and 97.8 mph. *Supercars Annual* covered the same distance in a Judge with Turbo Hydra-Matic transmission and racked up a run of 13.99 seconds at 107 mph!

By Brian Earnest

FIT FOR 'THE KING'

Pristine 1978 Eldorado has been locked in the dark since the day it left the dealer

This loaded 1978 Cadillac Eldorado Custom Biarritz was parked the day it left the dealership with 145 miles on the odometer. It never moved again until Dave Evans of Ashburn, Va., bought the car recently.

Dave Evans' uber-fancy 1978 Cadillac Eldorado Biarritz isn't just a car fit for a king.

It was a car built in honor of "The King" himself.

Elvis Presley left us back in August of 1977, and not long after his passing, a Tennessee woman who apparently worshipped the legendary crooner decided she needed a Cadillac to remember him by. Actually, she decided she needed a pair of them, so she ordered two loaded-to-the-gills 1978 Eldorado Biarritz Customs — a brown one and a brilliant white car with a red interior.

After getting the keys from Bill Gatton Chevrolet-Cadillac in Bristol, Tenn., the woman took the cars directly to the inspection station, then straight home to her garage. There, she parked the white Eldorado, with 145 miles on its odometer.

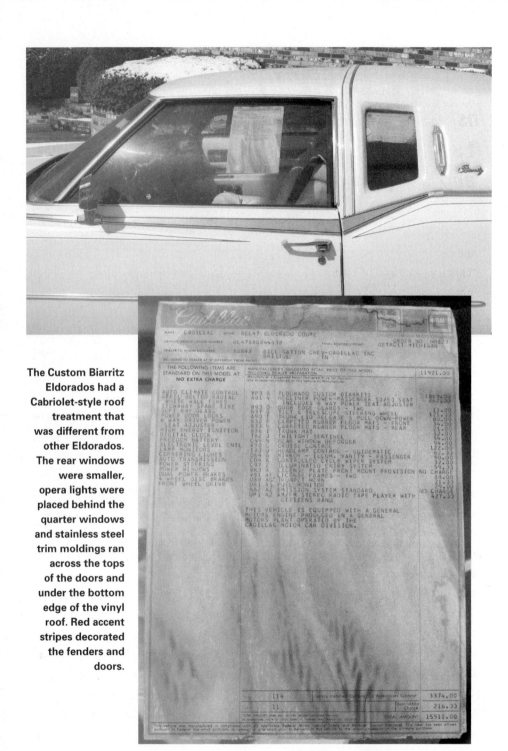

The Custom Biarritz Eldorados had a Cabriolet-style roof treatment that was different from other Eldorados. The rear windows were smaller, opera lights were placed behind the quarter windows and stainless steel trim moldings ran across the tops of the doors and under the bottom edge of the vinyl roof. Red accent stripes decorated the fenders and doors.

"It's unreal. The car has only 145 original miles. It drove from the dealer to the inspection station 86 miles, then to the house. It still has the dealer stickers on the window and there was never even a plate put on it."

And the car never moved again.

"There was 86 miles on the car when she did the inspection, and then they took the car home and parked it," Evans says incredulously. "That was the last time she ever drove it. Everybody has told me the car never moved again — her kids and everybody. Nobody ever drove the car.

"It actually belonged to my ex-girlfriend's parents," Evans added. "The lady died back in 1995 ... and last year the father was dying of cancer, and they were talking about this car in the garage they needed to sell. I asked if I could see it, and it was great! I couldn't believe it! It was scheduled to go to auction, but I said I wanted to buy the car, so I got it before it got to the public for auction.

"It's unreal. The car has only 145 original miles. It drove from the dealer to the inspection station 86 miles, then to the house. It still has the dealer stickers on the window and there was never even a plate put on it."

With its original oil in the engine, coolant in the radiator and air in the tires, the car was shipped to Moores Cadillac in Chantilly, Va., where mechanics have been "TLC-ing it for about three months," Evans said. The car still hasn't been started, but the old radiator core has been replaced, a leaking brake caliper has been fixed and a plastic filler piece between the passenger-side quarter panel and front bumper that broke when the car was moved is being replaced. The car hasn't even been cleaned up yet, but Evans said serious scrubbing isn't really necessary, even after 33 years. "Just sitting there, it looks like it doesn't even need washing," he said. "The sticker — I can't believe it was never even taken off the window. It's still got the paper floor mats on the floor."

Evans, a resident of Ashburn, Va., will never know for sure if the owner had planned to just keep the car as some kind of an expensive keepsake, or if she actually planned to drive it, but when she went car shopping, she went right for the top shelf. The Eldorado was as good as things got among American luxury cars at the time,

The Custom Biarritz included luxurious "pillowed" style leather or velour upholstery. This car was ordered with a red and white interior to match its exterior paint scheme. The original owner was a big Elvis Presley fan, according to current owner Dave Evans, and she ordered two Custom Biarritz Eldorados after Presley — a Cadillac fan himself — died in August of 1977.

and the Custom Biarritz package added a host of high-class goodies to an already ritzy machine. The Custom Biarritz group was available from 1977-'79 and included special color combinations, accent striping, a padded vinyl roof, special Biarritz badging and extra-plush interiors. Exterior paint options were Cotillion White, Colonial Yellow, Ruidoso Saddle, Carmine Red and Mediterranean Blue Firemist. Interiors were available in white, light blue, light yellow, medium saddle and dark carmine.

The quarter windows and rear window were different from other Eldorados, there

was special stainless-steel accent moldings that stretched horizontally along the tops of the doors and rear quarter panels, and special accent striping ran under the moldings. Special opera lamps were mounted behind the rear quarter windows and special decorative wheel covers were also part of the package. All of these extras tacked $1,865 onto the price of an Eldorado in 1978.

Not that the regular Eldorados weren't fancy enough. Standard equipment included a 425-cid, 180-hp V-8 with either fuel injection or carburetor, four-wheel disc brakes, front-wheel drive, electronic level control, automatic climate control, power windows and door locks, cornering lamps, six-way power seat, three-speed wipers, Freedom battery, lamp monitors, trip odometer, wide-whitewall steel-belted radial tires, Soft-Ray tinted glass, accent striping, remote control left-hand mirror, vanity mirror, lighters, bumper impact strips and a stowaway spare tire.

A revised crosshatch grille with heavier horizontal bars was seen on the front of 1978 Eldorados. The four-row peaked checkerboard grille was flanked by quad rectangular headlamps. Amber parking lamps sat low on the bumper. Large chrome vertical bumper ends extended upward around the auxiliary lamps. Options such as AM/FM stereo with tape player and CB radio, tilt/telescoping steering wheel, cruise control, rear window defogger, trumpet horn and trunk lid release ran the final bill on Evans' car to $15,511. "That's a pretty hefty price back then," Evans noted. "Fifteen-thousand dollars, and then just to park it?"

Cadillac's luxury coupe came only as a two-door and was base priced at $11,921 in 1978. At a whopping 4,906 lbs., the Eldorados were the heaviest cars in the Caddy lineup. A total of 46,816 were built, putting them fourth in line in popularity among Cadillacs behind the deVille coupe and sedan, Seville sedan and Fleetwood Brougham sedan.

About 2,000 Eldorado Biarritzes also received the "Classic" package, which included a power sunroof or "Astroroof" from American Sunroof in Southgate, Mich. A handful of the cars were also outfitted with special sliding power T-tops from American Sunroof. Some sources say seven of these T-top cars still exist.

It's a safe bet that Evans' Eldorado is the most pristine 1978 example on the planet. "It's still got the stubbies on the tires," he laughs. "It just sat in the garage, and the garage was built into the side of a mountain. It was all brick, with stone for the garage floor. It was just pitch black in there and nobody ever went in there.

"The lady that bought the car, she heard that Elvis had a white Cadillac with a red interior, and she had to have a car just like his. She was just crazy about Elvis, I guess. She even bought the same kind of casket Elvis Presley was buried in!... She died in 1995, and the family didn't do anything with the car. [Her husband] decided, 'No, we're not going to do anything with it, it's just going to sit there.' Nobody wanted it. The kids didn't want the car, nobody in the family wanted it, but I did! It's no Shelby Mustang, but it's still cool and really unique.

"After I bought it, it sat there for about six months because it was snowed in in the mountains, and when I got it to [Moores Cadillac in] Chantilly, the mechanic there was just beside himself. Everything on it is just amazing. The leather is perfect — it looks like a brand new car. The rooftop, the paint — it's all perfect. The guys from

Cadillac just couldn't believe the car sat that long."

Evans said he put in a new battery in the Cadillac and turned the key just enough to see if the starter would turn over, and everything seemed to work. He has not had the car running yet, but plans to do so soon. "I want to be there when we start it so I can hear it run," he said. "Right now, I just want to get it operational. We're just doing a little bit here and a little bit there. The plug wires are still soft. The belts and radiator hoses are all still soft. We haven't had to replace any of that. We're being real cautious with what we do."

More than anything, Evans said he knew he needed to get a hold of the car so it wouldn't end up with somebody who didn't fully appreciate the Eldorado's unmolested condition. "I just said, 'Wow, I have to have this car … I saw it and said, 'This cannot wind up in the wrong hands.' I'm not sure what will happen with it. It's up in the air. There's no way I'll drive it. I just can't see driving this car at this point. I'd be too afraid something would happen to it, with my luck.

"It should probably go to a collector who will hang onto it in a big warehouse or collection somewhere and not drive it."